Colorado
NOTARY PRIMER

The NNA's Handbook for Colorado Notaries

Thirteenth Edition

Published by:

National Notary Association
9350 De Soto Avenue
Chatsworth, CA 91311-4926
Telephone: (800) 876-6827
Fax: (818) 700-0920
Website: NationalNotary.org
Email: nna@NationalNotary.org

©2022 National Notary Association
ALL RIGHTS RESERVED. No part of this book may be reproduced in any form without permission in writing from the publisher.

The information in this *Primer* is correct and current at the time of its publication, although new laws, regulations and rulings may subsequently affect the validity of certain sections. This information is provided to aid comprehension of state Notary Public requirements and should not be construed as legal advice. Please consult an attorney for inquiries relating to legal matters.

Thirteenth Edition ©2022
First Edition ©2002

ISBN: 978-1-59767-293-1

Table of Contents

Introduction	1
Notary Laws Explained	2
The Notary Appointment	3
Screening the Signer	8
Checking the Document	15
Notary Acts	21
Recordkeeping	35
Notary Certificate and Stamp	39
Electronic and Remote Online Notarizations	44
Misconduct, Fines and Penalties	51
Colorado Laws Pertaining to Notaries Public	57
About the NNA	105
Index	106

Have a Tough Notary Question?

If you were a National Notary Association member, you could get the answer to that difficult question. Join the NNA® and your membership includes access to the NNA® Hotline* and live Notary experts providing the latest Notary information regarding laws, rules and regulations.

Hours
Monday – Friday   5:00 a.m.–7:00 p.m. (PT)
Saturday   5:00 a.m.–5:00 p.m. (PT)

NNA® Hotline Toll-Free Phone Number: 1-888-876-0827

After hours you can leave a message or email our experts at Hotline@NationalNotary.org and they will respond the next business day.

*Access to the NNA® Hotline is for National Notary Association members and NNA® Hotline subscribers only. Call and become a member today.

Introduction

You are to be commended on your interest in Colorado Notary law! Purchasing the *Colorado Notary Primer* identifies you as a conscientious professional who takes your official duties seriously.

In few fields is the expression "more to it than meets the eye" truer than in Notary law. What often appears on the surface to be a simple procedure may, in fact, have important legal considerations.

The purpose of the *Colorado Notary Primer* is to provide you with a resource to help decipher the many intricate laws that affect notarization. In so doing, the *Primer* will acquaint you with all of the important aspects of Colorado's Notary law and with prudent notarial practices in general.

The *Colorado Notary Primer* takes you through the myriad of Notary laws and puts them in easy-to-understand terms. Every section of the law is analyzed and explained, as well as topics not covered by Colorado law that are nonetheless of vital concern to you as a Notary. For your convenience, we have reprinted the complete text of the laws of Colorado that relate to Notaries Public.

Whether you are about to be appointed for the first time or are a longtime Notary, we are sure that the *Colorado Notary Primer* will provide you with new insight and understanding.

Milton G. Valera
Chairman
National Notary Association

Notary Laws Explained

In layperson's language, this chapter discusses and clarifies key parts of the laws of Colorado that regulate Notaries Public. Most of these laws are reprinted in full in "Colorado Laws Pertaining to Notaries Public," beginning on page 57.

In the text that follows, the following abbreviations are used:

- **CRS.** Colorado Revised Statutes, containing the enacted laws that regulate the activities of Notaries Public.

- **CCR.** Colorado Code of Regulations, containing the regulations that implement the Notary laws.

Additional information about Colorado requirements for Notaries Public is available on the Secretary of State's website. For step-by-step instructions on the commission application process, applicants also may visit NationalNotary.org/colorado/. ■

The Notary Appointment

Application for Appointment

Qualifications. To become a Notary Public in the state of Colorado, the applicant for a Notary commission must (CRS 24-21-251 [3][a-f]):

1. Be at least 18 years of age.
2. Be a resident or have a place of employment in the state of Colorado.
3. Never have been convicted of a felony, official misconduct or, in the past five years, a misdemeanor involving dishonesty.
4. Be able to read and write English.
5. Never have had a Notary commission revoked.
6. Be lawfully present in the United States.
7. Pass an examination.

Application Affirmation. Applicants must subscribe to the following affirmation, which is printed on the application available from the Secretary of State, in the presence of a Notary or other official authorized to administer oaths (CRS 24-21-521[5]):

I, _____ (name of applicant) solemnly affirm, under the penalty of perjury in the second degree, as defined in section 18-8-503, Colorado Revised Statutes, that I have carefully read the notary law of this state, and, if appointed and commissioned as a notary public, I will faithfully perform, to the best of my ability, all notarial acts in conformance with the law.

Application Fee. The fee for a Notary commission is $10 paid by credit or debit card during the online application procedure.

Required Training and Exam. An applicant who does not hold a commission in Colorado (including those whose previous commission has lapsed by more than 30 days), as well as renewing Notaries, must complete a state-approved Notary training program and must pass an examination administered by the Secretary of State (CRS 24-21-522 and CCR 2.1.2-3).

The Secretary of State also may require a Notary who has committed official misconduct to take an approved training program and pass the examination (CCR 2.1.5).

Lawful U.S. Residency Required. The Secretary of State is required to verify the lawful presence in the United States of any Notary commission applicant through verification procedures contained in CRS 24-76.5-103(4) (CRS 24-21-103[5]).

Verification of lawful presence requires presentation of a valid Colorado driver's license or a Colorado identification card, United States military card or a military dependent's identification card, United States Coast Guard Merchant Mariner card, or Native American tribal document, and execution of an affidavit stating that the person is a United States citizen or legal permanent resident, or that he or she is otherwise lawfully present in the United States pursuant to federal law.

Effective July 1, 2022, Colorado SB 21-199 expands on the existing requirement under Colorado law for the Secretary of State to check the lawful presence in the United States of every applicant for a commission by listing one of eight forms of identification an applicant may present or accepting an affidavit of the applicant stating they are residing lawfully in the United States.

Under this new law, the acceptable forms of identification for verifying lawful presence in the United States are: (i) a United States military card or a military dependent's identification card; (ii) a United States Coast Guard merchant mariner card; (iii) a Native American tribal document; (iv) a valid Colorado driver's license or a Colorado identification card (v) a valid driver's license or identification card issued by another state, the District of Columbia, Puerto Rico, the United States Virgin Islands, or any territory or insular possession subject to the jurisdiction of the United States that is compliant with the federal "Real ID Act", as amended; (vi) a valid United States passport; (vii) a valid United States permanent resident card; or (viii) any other valid type of identification that requires proof of lawful presence in the United States (CO SB 21-199).

Notary Bond

Not Required. Colorado Notaries are not required to obtain a surety bond.

Liability. A Notary Public and the surety or sureties on his or her bond are liable to the persons involved for all damages caused by the Notary's official misconduct (CRS 24-21-531[2]).

If a person is financially injured by a Notary's negligence or failure to properly execute a notarial act — whether performed intentionally or unintentionally — the Notary may be sued in civil court and ordered to pay all resulting damages, including attorney's fees (CRS 12-55-116).

A person need not be named in a document in order to sue a Notary for damages resulting from the Notary's handling of that document. If, for example, a lender accepts a forged, notarized deed as collateral for a loan, the lender might sue to recover losses from the Notary who notarized the signature on the fraudulent deed.

Errors and Omissions Insurance. Notaries may choose to purchase insurance to cover any unintentional errors or omissions they may make. Notary errors and omissions insurance provides protection for Notaries who are involved in claims or sued for damages resulting from unintentional notarial errors and omissions. In the event of a claim or civil lawsuit, the insurance company will provide and pay for the Notary's legal counsel and absorb any damages levied by a court or agreed to in a settlement, up to the policy coverage limit. Generally, errors and omissions insurance does not cover the Notary for dishonest, fraudulent or criminal acts or omissions, or for willful or intentional disregard of the law.

Colorado law gives Notaries the right to obtain insurance or a surety bond voluntarily to provide protection against lawsuits (CRS 24-21-531[3]).

Commission Recording

Optional. The Secretary of State issues a Certificate of Appointment qualifying the person as a Notary. Notaries may record the Certificate with a county clerk, however it is optional and rarely done. Upon recording the Certificate, the county clerk can issue an authentication certificate (CRS 12-55-109). (See "Authentication," page 19.)

Jurisdiction

Statewide. Notaries may perform official acts throughout the state of Colorado but not beyond the state borders. A Notary may not witness a signing outside Colorado and then return to the state to perform the notarization. All parts of a notarial act must be performed at the same time and place within the state.

Term of Office

Four-Year Term. A Colorado Notary Public's term of office is four years (CRS 24-21-521[6]).

Notarizing Without a Commission. A Notary who knowingly notarizes without a commission or after his or her commission expires commits a class 2 misdemeanor and may become ineligible for reappointment (CRS 24-21-523[1][k], CRS 24-21-532).

Reappointment

Not Automatic. Notaries will not be automatically reappointed at the end of the four-year term. A Notary who wishes to renew his or her commission may submit an application for reappointment before or at the expiration of the commission.

Change of Address or Name

If Notary Changes Address. A Notary who changes his or her residence or business address during the term of commission must notify the Secretary of State within 30 days (CRS 24-21-530).

If Notary Changes Name. A Notary whose name changes during the term of his or her commission must notify the Secretary of State within 30 days. A sample of the Notary's handwritten official signature must be included in the notice (CRS 24-21-530).

Resignation of Appointment

Notification. To resign, a Notary must notify the Secretary of State. Resignations may be filed electronically on the Secretary of State's website. A printable resignation form is also available from the "Forms" link on the website. Such a resignation is also mandatory if the Notary moves out of the state. The Notary must retain the journal for ten years after the last notarization recorded in the journal and notify the Secretary of State of the location of the journal. Or, instead of retaining the journal, the Notary can send the journal to the state archives or leave the journal with their firm or employer (CRS 24-21-519[10][A]). The Notary must also disable the stamping device rendering it unusable (CRS 24-21-518).

Death of Notary

Heirs Notify State. On the death or adjudication of incompetency of a current or former Notary Public, the Notary's personal representative or guardian or any other person knowingly in possession of the journal shall send the journal to the state archives and notify the Secretary of State in writing, and shall disable the stamp, rendering it unusable (CRS 24-21-518 [1]) and (CRS 24-21-519 [11]). ■

Screening the Signer

Personal Appearance

Requirement. The principal signer must personally appear before the Notary at the time of the notarization. This means that the Notary and the signer must be face-to-face when the notarization takes place. For traditional and in-person electronic notarizations, the Notary and signer must be physically present in the same room. For remote online notarizations, the Notary and signer must communicate via real-time, live, audio-video technology. Notarizations may never be performed over the telephone.

Willingness

Satisfaction. When performing a notarization, the Notary must be satisfied that the signer is not under duress or being coerced.

To satisfy themselves that signers are acting willingly, Notaries need only ask signers if they are signing of their own free will.

If a signer does or says anything that makes the Notary think the signer is being pressured to sign, the Notary must refuse to notarize.

Awareness

Assessment. A Notary has a duty to assess whether the signer has a basic comprehension of the document being signed. To assess a signer's awareness, the Notary simply makes a lay person's judgment about the signer's ability to understand what is taking place. According to the Colorado Notary Handbook, this assessment can be made by asking the client about the transaction, or just by asking the client what the document is and whether he/she agrees with it. If the signer's awareness is in doubt, the Notary must refuse to notarize.

Foreign-Language Signers. There should always be direct communication between the Notary and signer, whether in English or another language. The Notary must never rely upon an intermediary or interpreter to determine a signer's willingness or awareness. A third party may have reasons to misrepresent the transaction to the Notary and/or to the signer.

Identifying Document Signers

Requirement. In performing any notarial act, Colorado Notaries are required to positively identify the person requesting the notarization, based on either personal knowledge or satisfactory evidence (CRS 24-21-507) (CRS 24-21-507[2]).

Colorado law defines satisfactory evidence as either an identification document that meets certain criteria or the oath or affirmation of a third party who meets certain criteria. As a result, the following methods of identification are acceptable:

1. The Notary's *personal knowledge* of the signer's identity (see "Personal Knowledge of Identity," page 10);

2. The oath or affirmation of a personally known *credible identifying witness* (see "Credible Identifying Witness," pages 10–12); or

3. Reliable *identification documents* or ID cards (see "Acceptable as Identification," page 11).

Personal Knowledge of Identity

Definition. The safest and most reliable method of identifying a signer is for the Notary to depend upon his or her own personal knowledge of the signer's identity. Personal knowledge means familiarity with an individual resulting from interactions with that person over a period of time sufficient to eliminate every reasonable doubt that the person has the identity claimed.

Colorado law does not specify how long a Notary must be acquainted with an individual before personal knowledge of identity may be claimed. The Notary's common sense must prevail. In general, the longer the Notary is acquainted with a person, and the more interactions the Notary has had with that person, the more likely the individual is personally known.

For instance, the Notary might safely regard a friend since childhood as personally known, but would be foolish to consider a person met for the first time the previous day as such. Whenever the Notary has a reasonable doubt about a signer's identity, the identification should be made through either a credible identifying witness or reliable identification documents.

Credible Identifying Witness

Purpose. When a signer is not personally known to the Notary and is unable to present reliable ID cards, that signer may be identified on the oath of a credible identifying witness.

Qualifications. Every credible identifying witness must be personally known to the signer and to the Notary or identified by the Notary on the basis of a passport, driver's license, or government-issued nondriver identification that is current or expired not more than one year prior to the date of notarization (CRS 24-21-507[2][b]).

Any reliable credible identifying witness should have a reputation for honesty. The witness should be a competent individual who will not be tricked, bullied or otherwise influenced into identifying someone that he or she does not really know. Also, the witness should have no personal interest in the transaction requiring a notarial act.

Oath (Affirmation) for Credible Identifying Witness. An oath or affirmation should be administered to the credible identifying witness by the Notary to compel truthfulness.

An acceptable credible witness oath or affirmation might be:

> Do you solemnly swear you know that this signer is the person he/she claims to be, so help you God?
>
> (Do you solemnly affirm you know that this signer is the person he/she claims to be)?

Acceptable Identification. If a Notary cannot identify a signer by personal knowledge or through a mutually known credible identifying witness, the Notary may use an ID card to identify the signer. Such cards are considered to be "satisfactory evidence" of identity in lieu of personal knowledge, just as is the sworn word of a personally known credible identifying witness.

Colorado law specifies that an ID card must be current or expired less than one year, issued by a state or federal government, and contain a photograph or signature (CRS 24-21-507).

Examples of acceptable forms of identification include:

1. Colorado driver's license or official nondriver's ID. including the digital ID or digital driver's license (Executive Order B 2019 013).

2. Driver's license or official nondriver's ID issued by another state.

3. U.S. passport.

4. Foreign passport.

Multiple Identifications. While one acceptable identification document or card may be sufficient to identify a signer, the Notary may ask for more, especially if the Notary has a reasonable doubt as to the signer's identity or suspects that the signer has fraudulent identification.

Unacceptable Identification Documents. Identification documents that are not acceptable for identifying signers include Social Security cards, credit cards and birth certificates.

Fraudulent Identification. Identification documents are the least secure of the three methods of identifying a signer because phony IDs are common. The Notary should scrutinize each card for evidence of tampering or counterfeiting, or for evidence that it is a genuine card that has been issued to an impostor.

Some clues that an ID card may have been fraudulently altered include mismatched type styles, a photograph raised from the surface, a signature that does not match the signature on the document, unauthorized lamination of the card, and smudges, erasures, smears and discolorations.

Possible tip-offs to a counterfeit ID card include misspelled words, a brand-new-looking card with an old date of issuance, two cards with exactly the same photograph, and inappropriate patterns and textures. Indications that an identification card may have been issued to an impostor include the birthdate or address on the card being unfamiliar to the bearer and all the ID cards seeming brand new.

Signature by Mark

Purpose. A person who cannot sign his or her name because of illiteracy or a physical disability may instead use a mark — an "X" for example — as a signature.

Witnesses. For a signature by mark to be notarized, the National Notary Association recommends that there be two witnesses to the making of the mark. The witnesses should sign the document or electronic record, and one witness should write the marker's name beside the mark.

A mark should also be affixed in the Notary's journal, and the witnesses should sign the journal as well.

Notarization Procedures. The marker must be positively identified, just like any other signer. Because a properly witnessed mark is regarded as a signature by custom and law, the Notary is not required to use any other special procedures or certificates.

Signature by Proxy

Principal Directing Another Person to Sign. A person unable to sign or make a mark can direct someone other than the Notary to sign the person's name on the document, provided (CRS 24-21-509[1]):

1. The principal, in the Notary's presence, directs the other person to sign the principal's name or to attach the principal's electronic signature.

2. The words "Signature written by (name of individual directed to sign) at the direction and in the presence of (name as signed) on whose behalf the signature was written" or substantially similar wording should appear under or near the signature. If an electronic signature is used, the words "Signature attached by" can be substituted for "Signature written by," and the words "attached electronically" can be used in place of "written."

Alternative Communication Methods

Unable to Speak or Write. If an individual appears to the Notary to be unable to speak or write, the Notary may use signals or electronic or mechanical means to communicate, take an acknowledgment or execute an oath or affirmation (CRS 24-21-509[2]).

Notarizing for Minors

Under Age 18. Generally, persons must reach the age of majority before they can handle their own legal affairs and sign documents for themselves. In Colorado, the age of majority is 18. Normally, parents or guardians will sign on a minor's behalf. In certain cases, where minors are engaged in business transactions or serving as court witnesses, they may lawfully sign documents and have their signatures notarized.

Include Age Next to Signature. When notarizing for a minor, the Notary should ask the young signer to write his or her age next to the signature to alert any person relying upon the document that the signer is a minor. The Notary is not required to verify the minor signer's age.

Identification. The method for identifying a minor is the same as that for an adult. Because minors often do not possess acceptable identification documents, such as driver's licenses or passports, determining the identity of a minor can be a problem. If the minor does not have an acceptable ID, then the other methods of identification must be used: either the Notary's personal knowledge of the minor or the oath of a credible identifying witness who can identify the minor. (See "Identifying Document Signers," page 9.) ■

Checking the Document

Blank or Incomplete Documents

Do Not Notarize. Colorado law prohibits notarizing a document that is blank or contains blank spaces (CRS 24-21-525[7]). This is a dangerous practice, similar to signing a blank check.

A fraudulent document could easily be created above a Notary's signed and stamped certificate on an otherwise blank paper. Additionally, with documents containing blanks to be filled in after the notarization by a person other than the signer, there is a danger that the information inserted will be contrary to the wishes of the signer.

Any blanks in a document may be filled in by the signer prior to notarization. If the blanks are inapplicable and intended to be left unfilled, the signer should line through each space or write "Not Applicable" or "N/A." The Notary may not, however, tell the signer what to write in the blanks. If the signer is unsure how to complete the blanks, he or she should contact the document's issuer, its eventual recipient or an attorney.

Refusal of Service

Discrimination. Notaries should honor all lawful and reasonable requests to notarize. A person's race, age, gender, religion, nationality, ethnicity, lifestyle or political viewpoint is never legitimate cause for refusing to perform a notarial act.

Reasonable Care

Responsibility. As public servants, Notaries must act responsibly and exercise reasonable care in the performance of their official duties. If a Notary fails to do so, he or she may be subject to a civil suit to recover financial damages caused by the Notary's error.

In general, reasonable care is that degree of concern and attentiveness that a person of normal intelligence and responsibility would exhibit.

Complying with all pertinent laws is the first rule of reasonable care for a Notary. If there are no statutory guidelines in a given instance, the Notary should exercise common sense.

Disqualifying Interest

Impartiality. Notaries are appointed by the state to be impartial, disinterested witnesses whose screening duties help ensure the integrity of important transactions. Lack of impartiality by a Notary throws doubt on the integrity and lawfulness of any transaction. A Notary must never notarize his or her own signature, nor notarize in a transaction in which the Notary has a disqualifying interest. The Notary has a disqualifying interest if the Notary or the Notary's spouse, partner in a civil union, ancestor, descendant, or sibling is a party to or is named in the document (CRS 24-21-504[2][a]).

Financial or Beneficial Interest. Colorado Notaries may not notarize any instrument in which the Notary has a disqualifying interest. Such an interest exists when the Notary or the Notary's spouse or partner in a civil union may receive directly, and as a result of the notarization, any advantage, right, title interest, cash or property exceeding the maximum notary fee (CRS 24-21-504[2][B]).

Relatives. A Colorado Notary cannot notarize a document if a spouse, partner in a civil union, ancestor, descendant, or sibling is a party to or is named in the document (CRS 24-21-504[2][a]).

Unauthorized Practice of Law

Do Not Assist Others with Legal Matters. As a ministerial officer, the nonattorney Notary is not permitted to assist other persons in drafting or giving legal advice about documents or immigration matters, and cannot represent a person in any preceding relating to immigration matters, or receive compensation for performing an unauthorized practice of law (CRS 24-21-525[1][a-d]).

A Notary, of course, may fill in the blanks on the Notary certificate. And a Notary, as a private individual, may prepare legal documents that he or she is personally a party to, but the Notary may not notarize his or her signature on these same documents.

Notaries who overstep their authority by advising others on legal matters may be prosecuted for the unauthorized practice of law and have their commissions revoked.

Exceptions. Nonattorney Notaries who are specially trained, certified or licensed in a particular field such as real estate, insurance or escrow may advise others about documents in that field, but in no other. In addition, trained paralegals under the supervision of an attorney may advise others about documents in routine legal matters.

Foreign-Language Documents. Although Colorado Notaries are not expressly prohibited from notarizing documents written in a language they cannot read, there are difficulties and dangers in doing so: The document may be misrepresented to the Notary, a blatant fraud may go undetected, the Notary may inadvertently perform an incorrect or illegal notarial act, and making a complete journal entry may be difficult.

Ideally, a foreign-language document should be referred to a Notary who reads that language. In many states, the website of the Notary-regulating official has a Notary directory. These directories often include the foreign languages read or spoken by each Notary listed.

If a Notary chooses to notarize a document that he or she cannot read, then the Notary certificate should be in English or in a language the Notary can read, and the signature being notarized should be written in characters the Notary is familiar with.

Wills

Authorized Formality. Colorado law allows Notaries to perform an acknowledgment of a signer's signature on a will (CRS 5-11-502[1][c][II]).

Do Not Offer Advice. Often, people attempt to draw up wills on their own without benefit of legal counsel and then bring these homemade testaments to a Notary to have them "legalized," expecting the Notary to know how to proceed. In advising or assisting such persons, the Notary risks prosecution for the unauthorized practice of law. The Notary's ill-informed advice may do considerable damage to the affairs of the signer and subject the Notary to a civil lawsuit.

A Notary should notarize a will only if a Notary certificate is provided and the signer is not asking questions about how to proceed. The Notary should refer all questions to an attorney.

Self-Proving Wills. Typically, self-proven wills shorten and simplify the probate process. A will or codicil (amendment to a will) may be self-proved before a Notary at the time of its execution or any time thereafter with the acknowledgment of the testator and affidavits of two witnesses (CRS 15-11-504). A self-proving will that contains the notarized attestations of the testator and witnesses is recognized as an authentic will by the probate court when the will is filed without requiring the witnesses to appear in court to testify to the execution of the will.

Living Wills. Documents popularly called living wills may be notarized. These are not actually wills, but written statements of the signer's wishes concerning medical treatment in the event that the person is unable to issue instructions on his or her own behalf.

Immigration

Do Not Give Advice. Notaries may never advise others on the subject of immigration, nor help others prepare immigration documents — and especially not for a fee. Notaries who offer immigration advice to others may be prosecuted for the unauthorized practice of law and have their commissions revoked (CRS 24-21-525[1][b]).

Documents. While notaries may not offer advice on immigration matters, they may notarize immigration documents. Non-USCIS documents are often notarized and submitted in support of an immigration or naturalization petition. These might include translator's declarations, statements from employers and banks, and affidavits of relationship.

Authentication

Documents Sent out of State. Documents notarized in Colorado and sent out of state may be required to bear proof that the Notary's signature and stamp are genuine and that the Notary had authority to act at the time of notarization. This process of proving the genuineness of an official signature and stamp is called authentication or legalization.

Authenticating certificates for Colorado Notaries may be obtained at the Secretary of State's office.

Authenticating certificates may also be available from county clerks' offices where the Notary's commission has been filed.

These authenticating certificates are known by many different names: certificates of official character, certificates of authority, certificates of capacity, certificates of prothonotary and "flags."

Anyone who requires a certificate of authority should contact the Secretary of State's office. It is not the responsibility of the Notary Public to obtain authentication.

Documents Sent out of Country. If a notarized document will be sent out of the United States, a chain-authentication process may be necessary and certificates of authority may have to be obtained from the county clerk, the Colorado Secretary of State, the U.S. Department of State and different ministries of the involved foreign nation, here and abroad. This chain-certification process can be time-consuming and expensive.

***Apostilles* and the Hague Convention.** Fortunately, more than 100 nations, including the United States, subscribe to a treaty under auspices of the Hague Conference that simplifies authentication of notarized documents exchanged between any of these nations.

The official name of this treaty, adopted by the Convention on October 5, 1961, is *The Hague Convention Abolishing the Requirement of Legalization for Foreign Public Documents.* (For a list of the subscribing countries, visit hcch.net/index_en.php.)

Under the Hague Convention, only one authenticating certificate, called an *apostille*, is necessary to ensure acceptance of a Notary signature and stamp in subscribing countries. In Colorado, *apostilles* are issued by the Secretary of State.

Photocopies & Faxes

Original Signature. A photocopy or fax may be notarized as long as the signature on it is original, meaning that the photocopy or fax must have been signed with pen and ink. Signatures on documents presented for notarization must always be signed with a handwritten, original signature. A photocopied or faxed signature may never be notarized.

Public recorders sometimes will not accept notarized photocopies or faxes because the text of the document may be too faint to adequately reproduce in microfilming.

Notary Acts

Authorized Acts

Notaries may perform the following notarial acts (CRS 12-55-102 and 12-55-110):

- **Acknowledgments,** certifying that a signer personally appeared before the Notary, was identified by the Notary, and freely acknowledged signing the document. (See pages 22–24.)

- **Oaths and Affirmations,** solemn promises to a Supreme Being (oaths) or on one's own personal honor (affirmations) spoken in the Notary's presence. (See pages 24–26.)

- **Copy Certifications,** declaring that one or more copies are true and exact reproductions of originals. (See pages 26–27.)

- **Depositions and Affidavits,** the oral or written testimony of a witness or other person taken under oath or affirmation. (See pages 27–28.)

- **Verification on Oath or Affirmation (Jurats),** as found in affidavits and other sworn documents, certifying that a signer personally appeared before the Notary, took an oath or affirmation from the Notary, and signed the document in the Notary's presence. (See pages 28–29.)

- **Signature Witnessing**, when an individual appears before a Notary and signs a document in the Notary's presence. (See pages 29–30.)
- **Proofs of Execution**, certifying that a subscribing witness personally appeared and swore to the Notary that another person, the principal, signed a document. (See pages 30–32.)
- **Protests**, certifying that a written promise to pay, such as a bill of exchange, was not honored.

Unauthorized Acts

Marriages. Colorado Notaries are not authorized to perform marriages unless they also are members of the clergy or an official authorized to solemnize marriages.

Acknowledgments

Common Notarial Act. Acknowledgments are one of the most common forms of notarization.

Purpose. In executing an acknowledgment, the Notary certifies three things (CRS 12-55-205):

1. The signer *personally appeared* before the Notary on the date and in the county indicated on the Notary certificate (notarization cannot be based upon a telephone call or upon a Notary's familiarity with a signature).

2. The signer was *positively identified* by the Notary through personal knowledge or other satisfactory evidence (see "Identifying Document Signers," page 9).

3. The signer *acknowledged* to the Notary that the signature was freely made for the purposes stated in the document and, if the document is signed in a representative capacity, that he or she had proper authority to do so. (If a document is willingly signed in the presence of the Notary, this act can serve just as well as an oral statement of acknowledgment.)

Representative Capacity. A person may sign and acknowledge a document in a representative capacity on behalf of another person or a legal entity. Specifically, a representative capacity means (CRS 12-55-207):

- For and on behalf of a corporation, partnership, trust, or other entity as an authorized officer, agent, partner, trustee or other representative.

- As a public officer, personal representative, guardian or other representative in the specific capacity described in the document.

- As an attorney in fact for an absent principal signer.

- Or as an authorized representative of another person in any other lawful capacity (e.g., trustee, guardian, etc.).

Certificate Wording. Colorado statute provides the following short-form wording for an Acknowledgment by Individual and an Acknowledgment in a Representative Capacity:

- Acknowledgment by Individual (CRS 24-21-516[a]):

    State of _____
    County of _____

    This record was acknowledged before me on _____ (date) by _____ (name of individual(s)).

    (Signature of notarial officer)   (Stamp)
    (Title of office)
    My commission expires: _____

- Acknowledgment in a Representative Capacity (CRS 24-21-516[b]):

    State of _____
    County of _____

This record was acknowledged before me on _____ (date) by _____ (name of individual(s)) as _____ (type of authority, such as officer or trustee) of _____ (name of party on behalf of whom record was executed).

(Signature of notarial officer) (Stamp)

(Title of office)

My commission expires: _____

Identification of Acknowledger. In executing an acknowledgment, the Notary must identify the signer through personal knowledge or satisfactory evidence (CRS 12-55-205). (See "Identifying Document Signers," page 9.)

It is recommended that if a person is signing in a representative capacity that the Notary verify that authority (i.e., if the signer is signing as attorney in fact, the signer could present the Power of Attorney).

Signing in Notary's Presence Not Required. For an acknowledgment, the document does not have to be signed in the Notary's presence. Rather, the signer need only acknowledge having made the signature. As long as the signer appears before the Notary at the time of notarization to acknowledge having signed, the Notary may execute the acknowledgment.

The document could have been signed an hour before, a week before, a year before, etc., as long as the signer appears before the Notary with the signed document at the time of notarization to admit that the signature is his or her own.

Oaths and Affirmations

Purpose. An oath is a solemn, spoken pledge to a Supreme Being. An affirmation is a solemn, spoken pledge on one's own personal honor, with no reference to a Supreme Being. Both are usually a promise of truthfulness and have the same legal effect.

In taking an oath or affirmation in an official proceeding, a person may be subject to criminal penalties for perjury should he or she fail to be truthful.

An oath or affirmation can be a full-fledged notarial act in its own right, as when administering an oath of office to a public official, or it can be part of the process of notarizing a document (executing a jurat, swearing in a credible identifying witness, etc.). A person who objects to taking an oath may instead be given an affirmation.

Power to Administer. Notaries may administer any oath or affirmation required by state law (CRS 12-55-110).

Wording for Oath (Affirmation). CO House Bill 18-1138 creates a uniform and standardized oath of office for all public officials and positions. This oath is required to be in writing and signed by the person taking the oath or affirmation. However, state law does not prescribe specific wording for other verbal oaths and affirmations. A Notary may use the following or similar words in administering an oath (or affirmation):

- Oath (Affirmation) for an affiant signing an affidavit or a deponent signing a deposition:

    Do you solemnly swear that the statements made in this affidavit (or deposition) are the truth, the whole truth, and nothing but the truth, so help you God?

    (Do you solemnly affirm that the statements made in this affidavit [or deposition] are the truth, the whole truth, and nothing but the truth?)

- Oath (Affirmation) for a credible identifying witness identifying a signer who is in the Notary's presence:

    Do you solemnly swear that you know this signer truly is the person he/she claims to be, so help you God?

    (Do you solemnly affirm that you know this signer truly is the person he/she claims to be?)

Response Required. The oath or affirmation wording must be spoken aloud, and the person taking the oath or affirmation must answer affirmatively with "I do," "Yes," or the like. A nod or grunt is not a sufficient response. If a person is unable to speak, the Notary may rely upon other means to communicate (CRS 12-55-110.5).

Ceremony and Gestures. To impress upon the person taking the oath or affirmation the importance of truthfulness, the Notary may lend a sense of ceremony to the oath or affirmation by asking the person taking the oath or affirmation to raise his or her right hand, though this is not a legal requirement. Notaries generally have discretion to use the words and gestures that they feel will most compellingly appeal to the conscience of the person taking the oath or affirmation.

Oaths Are Personal. Only an individual may take an oath or affirmation. A "corporation" or "partnership" may not take an oath or affirmation, but an individual representing a corporation, partnership or other legal entity may take an oath or affirmation as an individual, swearing that he or she has authority to sign for that entity.

Copy Certifications

Purpose. Colorado Notaries have the authority to certify that a copy of a record or an item is a full, true, and accurate transcription or reproduction of the record or item" (CRS 24-21-505[4][a]).

Procedure. The person requesting the certified copy must present the document or item to the Notary and request a certified copy.

The Notary must make or closely supervise the making of the photocopy to ensure that it is true, exact and unaltered.

Prohibited Documents. A Notary may not certify a copy of a record that can be obtained from any of the following offices (CRS 24-21-505[4][b]):

1. A clerk and recorder of public documents
2. The secretary of state
3. The state archives
4. An office of vital records

A Notary is also prohibited from providing copy certifications for documents that state on their face that it is illegal to make copies of them (CRS 24-21-505[4][c]).

Certificate Wording. Colorado statute provides the following short-form wording for copy certification (CRS 24-21-516[e]):

State of _____

County of _____

I certify that this is a true and correct copy of a record in the possession of _____.

Dated _____

(Signature of notarial officer)   (Stamp)

(Title of office)

My commission expires: _____

Depositions and Affidavits

Purpose. A deposition is a signed transcript of the signer's oral statement taken down for use in a judicial proceeding. This deposition signer is called a deponent.

An affidavit is a signed statement made under oath or affirmation by a person called an affiant, and it is used for a variety of purposes, both in and out of court.

For both a deposition and an affidavit, the Notary must administer an oath or affirmation and complete some form of jurat, which the Notary signs and stamps.

Depositions. With a deposition, both sides in a lawsuit or court case have the opportunity to cross-examine the deponent. Questions and answers are transcribed into a written statement. Used only in judicial proceedings, a deposition is then signed and sworn to before an oath-administering official.

Colorado Notaries have the power to take depositions — meaning, to transcribe the words spoken aloud by a deponent — but this duty is most often executed by trained and certified court reporters.

Affidavits. Affidavits are used in and out of court for a variety of purposes, from declaring losses to an insurance company to declaring U.S. citizenship before traveling to a foreign country. An affidavit is a document containing a statement voluntarily signed and sworn to or affirmed before a Notary or other official with oath-administering powers. If used in a judicial proceeding, only one side in the case need participate in the execution of the affidavit, unlike with the deposition.

Oath (Affirmation) for Depositions and Affidavits. If no other wording is prescribed in a given instance, a Notary may use the following language in administering an oath (affirmation) for an affidavit or deposition:

> Do you solemnly swear that the statements made in this affidavit (or deposition) are the truth, the whole truth, and nothing but the truth, so help you God?
>
> (Do you solemnly affirm that the statements made in this affidavit [or deposition] are the truth, the whole truth, and nothing but the truth?)

Verification on Oath or Affirmation (Jurat)

Purpose. While the purpose of an acknowledgment is to positively identify a signer, the purpose of a verification on oath or affirmation is to compel truthfulness by appealing to the signer's conscience and fear of criminal penalties for perjury.

In executing a verification on oath or affirmation, a Notary certifies that:

1. The signer *personally appeared* before the Notary at the time of notarization on the date and in the county indicated (notarization based upon a telephone call or on familiarity with a signature is not acceptable).

2. The signer was *positively identified* by the Notary through personal knowledge or other satisfactory evidence. (See "Identifying Document Signers," page 9.)

3. The Notary *watched the signer sign the document.*

4. The Notary *administered an oath or affirmation* to the signer.

Certificate Wording. Colorado statute provides the following short-form wording for verification on oaths or affirmations (CRS 24-21-516[c]):

> State of _____
>
> County of _____
>
> Signed and sworn to (or affirmed) before me on _____ (date) by _____ (name of individual(s) making statement).
>
> (Signature of notarial officer)   (Stamp)
>
> (Title of office)
>
> My commission expires: _____

Wording for Verification on Oath or Affirmation. If not otherwise prescribed by law, a Colorado Notary may use the following or similar wording to administer an oath (or affirmation) in conjunction with a jurat:

> Do you solemnly swear that the statements made in this document are the truth, the whole truth, and nothing but the truth, so help you God?
>
> (Do you solemnly affirm that the statements in this document are the truth, the whole truth, and nothing but the truth?)

Signature Witnessing

Purpose. The act of witnessing — or "attesting" — a signature may be used in circumstances in which the date of signing is of crucial importance. A signature witnessing differs from an acknowledgment in that the party relying upon the document may know that the document was signed on a certain date. A signature witnessing differs from a verification upon oath or affirmation in that the signer is merely signing the document in the presence of the Notary, not vouching that the contents of the document are true.

In witnessing or attesting a signature, the Notary certifies that (CRS 24-21-505[3]):

1. The signer personally appeared before the Notary on the date and in the county indicated on the Notary certificate.
2. The Notary positively identified the signer by personal knowledge or satisfactory evidence.
3. The signer affixed the signature in the presence of the Notary.

Certificate. A Notary may use the following short-form certificate for witnessing or attesting a signature (CRS 24-21-516[d]):

State of _____

County of _____

Signed before me on _____ (date) by _____ (name of individual(s)).

(Signature of notarial officer)   (Stamp)

(Title of office)

My commission expires: _____

Proof of Execution by Subscribing Witness

Purpose. In executing a proof of execution, a Notary certifies that the signature of a person who does not appear before the Notary — the principal signer — is genuine and freely made based upon the sworn testimony of another person who does appear: a subscribing (signing) witness.

Proofs of execution are used when the principal signer is out of town or otherwise unavailable to appear before a Notary. Because of their high potential for fraud, proofs should only be used as a last resort and never merely because the principal prefers not to take the time to appear before a Notary.

In Lieu of Acknowledgment. Proofs of execution by subscribing witness are permitted with any deed or instrument that has been signed but not acknowledged before a Notary or other official with notarial powers (CRS 38-30-136).

Subscribing Witness. A subscribing witness is a person who watches a principal sign a document (or who personally takes the principal's acknowledgment) and then subscribes (signs) his or her own name on the document at the principal's request.

State law does not provide or prescribe a specific form. However, the National Notary Association recommends the following certificate:

State of _____)
) ss.
County of _____)

On _____ (date), before me, the undersigned, a Notary Public for the state, personally appeared _____ (subscribing witness's name), personally known to me (or proved to me on the oath of _____ [credible identifying witness's name], who is personally known to me), to be the person whose name is subscribed to the within instrument, as a witness thereto, who, being by me duly sworn, deposed and said that he/she was present and saw _____ (name[s] of principal[s]), the same person(s) described in and whose name(s) is/are subscribed to the within and annexed instrument in his/her/their authorized capacity(ies) as (a) party(ies) thereto, execute the same, and that said affiant subscribed his/her name to the within instrument as a witness at the request of _____ (name[s] of principal[s]).

WITNESS my hand and official seal.

_____ (Signature of Notary)   (Seal of Notary)
_____ (Commission Expiration Date)

This witness brings that document to a Notary on the principal's behalf and takes an oath or affirmation from the Notary to vouch that the principal did willingly sign (or acknowledge signing) the document and requested the witness to also sign the document.

Identifying Subscribing Witness. The Notary must personally know the subscribing witness or the witness's identity must be proven by the oath of one credible identifying witness who is personally known to the Notary (CRS 38-30-136). (See "Credible Identifying Witness," page 10.)

The ideal subscribing witness is objective and impartial, and has no beneficial interest in the document or transaction. It would be foolish of the Notary, for example, to rely upon the word of a subscribing witness presenting for notarization a power of attorney that names this very witness as attorney in fact.

Oath (Affirmation) for Subscribing Witness. An acceptable oath for the subscribing witness might be:

> Do you solemnly swear that you saw (name of the document signer) sign his/ her name to this document and/or that he/she acknowledged to you having executed it for the purposes therein stated, so help you God?
>
> (Do you solemnly affirm that you saw [name of the document signer] sign his/ her name to this document and/or that he/she acknowledged to you having executed it for the purposes therein stated?)

The subscribing witness then signs the Notary's journal and the Notary completes the proof of execution by subscribing witness certificate, often called a witness jurat.

Certificate for Proof of Execution. Once the subscribing witness's identity has been proven, Colorado law requires that a certificate for a proof of execution by a subscribing witness be attached to the document (CRS 38-30-136).

Execution and Recordation Without Proof. If a document is notarized and recorded without due proof, attestation, or acknowledgment as required by law and subsequently lost or destroyed, a certified copy of the document may be acknowledged or proved by a subscribing witness in the same manner as the original. The certified copy will carry the same legal weight as the original document, but it cannot be used as an original unless the original is lost or destroyed (CRS 38-30-136).

Fees for Notary Services

Maximum Fees. The following maximum fees for performing notarial acts are allowed by Colorado law (CRS 24-21-529):

- **Acknowledgments — $5.** For taking an acknowledgment (including identifying the signer and completing the certificate) the Notary may charge no more than $5 for each document attested per signer.

- **Oaths and Affirmations — $5.** For administering an oath or affirmation as a notarial act in its own right and not incidental to a notarial act, the Notary may charge no more than $5 for each person taking the oath or affirmation.

- **Certified Copies — $5.** For certifying a copy of a document, the Notary may charge no more than $5 for each document certified.

- **Certified Copy of Journal Entry — $5.** For certifying a copy of an entry or entries from the Notary's journal, the Notary may charge no more than $5 for each copy certified.

- **Verification on Oath or Affirmation (Jurat) — $5.** For executing a jurat (including administering the oath or affirmation and completing the certificate) on an affidavit, deposition or other sworn, written statement, the Notary may charge no more than $5 for each document attested per signer.

- **Signature Witnessing — $5.** For witnessing the signature of a signer, the Notary may charge no more than $5 per signer.

- **Electronic Notarizations — $10.** For the Notary's electronic signature, the Notary may charge no more than $10.

Option Not to Charge. Notaries are not required to charge for their notarial services, and they may charge less than the maximum fee.

Travel Fees. Travel fees are proper only if the Notary and signer agree beforehand on the amount to be charged. The Notary should explain to the signer that a travel fee is not stipulated in law and is separate from the fees for notarization.

Advertising

False or Misleading Advertising. Misleading advertising that claims authority or power not granted to a Notary is prohibited by law (CRS 24-21-523[1][f]), (CRS 24-21-525[2,4-5]).

Notario Publico. A Notary, other than an attorney licensed to practice law in Colorado, may not use the term *'notario'* or *'notario publico'''* (CRS 24-21-525[3]).

Prohibited Representation. A Notary, other than an attorney licensed to practice law in Colorado, may not advertise or represent that he or she can assist in drafting legal records, give legal advice or otherwise practice law (CRS 24-21-525[4]).

Required Statement. If a Notary who is not an attorney licensed to practice law in this state in any manner advertises or represents that the Notary offers notarial services, whether orally or in a record, including broadcast media, print media, and the internet, the Notary must include the following statement, or an alternate statement authorized or required by the secretary of state, in the advertisement or representation, prominently and in each language used in the advertisement or representation: 'I am not an attorney licensed to practice law in the state of Colorado and I may not give legal advice or accept fees for legal advice. I am not an immigration consultant, nor am I an expert on immigration matters. If you suspect fraud, you may contact the Colorado attorney general's office or the Colorado supreme court.' If the form of advertisement or representation is not broadcast media, print media, or the internet and does not permit inclusion of the statement because of size, it must be displayed prominently or provided at the place of performance of the notarial act before the notarial act is performed" (CRS 24-21-525[4]). ■

Recordkeeping

Journal of Notarial Acts

Required. Colorado Notaries are required to keep an official journal of all notarial acts performed and, if required, provide a certified copy of any of the Notary's acts upon payment of the Notary's fee (CRS 24-21-519[1][5]).

Records of Notary Employee. Instead of maintaining a journal, a Notary may maintain the original or a copy, including an electronic record, of a document that contains the information otherwise required to be entered in the Notary's journal if the Notary's firm or employer retains the original, copy, or electronic record in the regular course of business (CRS 24-21-519[10][c]).

However, the Secretary of State contends that it is not in the best interest of the Notary to rely on this exception and strongly encourages notaries to keep records of all official acts (Notary Handbook).

Prudent Notaries keep detailed and accurate journals of all their notarial acts for many reasons:

- Keeping records is a businesslike practice that every conscientious businessperson and public official should engage in. Not keeping records of important transactions, whether private or public, is risky.

- A Notary's journal protects the public's rights to valuable property and to due process by providing documentary evidence in the event that a document is lost or altered, or if a transaction is later challenged.

- In the event of a civil lawsuit alleging the Notary's negligence or misconduct caused the plaintiff serious financial harm, a detailed journal of notarial acts can protect the Notary by showing that the Notary used reasonable care to identify a signer. It would be difficult to contend that the Notary did not bother to identify a signer if the Notary's journal contains a detailed description of the ID cards that the signer presented.

- Since civil lawsuits arising from a contested notarial act typically take place three to six years after the act occurs, the Notary normally cannot accurately testify in court about the particulars of a notarization without a journal to aid the Notary's memory.

- Journals of notarial acts prevent baseless lawsuits by showing that a Notary used reasonable care or a transaction occurred as recorded.

- Requiring each signer to leave a signature, or even a thumbprint, in the Notary's journal deters attempted forgeries and provides strong evidence for a conviction should a forgery occur.

Permanent Bound Journal. If a journal is maintained on a tangible medium, it must be a permanent, bound register with numbered pages. If it is maintained in an electronic format, it must be in a permanent, tamper-evident format (CRS 24-21-519[2]).

Journal Entries. The Notary's journal entries must be made at the same time as the notarization and contain the following information for each notarial act (CRS 24-21-519[3][A-G]):

1. The date and time of notarial act.
2. A description of the record, if any, and type of notarial act.
3. The full name and address of each individual for whom the notarial act is performed.

4. The signature or electronic signature of each individual for whom the notarial act is performed.

5. If identity is based on personal knowledge, a statement to that effect.

6. • If identity is based on satisfactory evidence, a brief description of the method of identification and type of identification card, if any.

7. The fee, if any, charged by the notary.

8. For all electronic records on documents signed using the Notary's electronic signature, the document authentication number issued by the Secretary of State must be included. (See "Electronic and Remote Online Notarizations," pages 44–50.)

Document Dates. If the document has a specific date on it, the Notary should record that date in the journal of notarial acts.

Often the only date on a document is the date of the signature that is being notarized. If the signature is undated, however, the document may have no date on it at all. In that case, the Notary should record "no date" or "undated" in the journal.

For acknowledgments, the date the document was signed must either precede or be the same as the date of the notarization; it may not follow it. For a verification on oath or affirmation, the date the document was signed and the date of the notarization must be the same.

A document whose signature is dated after the date on its Notary certificate risks rejection by a recorder, who may question how the document could have been notarized before it was signed.

Journal Signature. Perhaps the most important entry to obtain is the signer's signature. A journal signature protects the Notary against claims that a signer did not appear and is a deterrent to forgery because it provides evidence of the signer's identity and appearance before the Notary.

To check for possible forgery, the Notary should compare the

Recordkeeping | 37

signature that the person leaves in the journal of notarial acts with the signatures on the document and on the IDs presented. The signatures should be at least reasonably similar.

The Notary also should observe the signing of the journal. If the signer appears to be laboring over the journal signature, this may be an indication of forgery in progress.

Journal Thumbprint. Colorado law does not require a Notary to obtain a signer's thumbprint for the journal. However, many Notaries are asking document signers to leave a thumbprint in the journal. The journal thumbprint protects the Notary against claims that a signer did not appear and is a strong deterrent to forgery, because it represents absolute proof of the signer's identity and appearance before the Notary.

Provided the signer is willing, nothing prevents a Notary from asking for a thumbprint for every notarial act.

Since a thumbprint is not required by law, however, the Notary may not refuse to notarize if the signer declines to leave one.

Complete Entry Before Certificate. The prudent Notary completes the journal entry before filling out the Notary certificate on a document. This prevents the signer from leaving with the notarized document before vital information can be entered in the journal.

Never Surrender Journal. A Notary is responsible for the security of the journal and shall keep it in a secure area under the exclusive control of the notary and shall not allow any other notary to use the journal (CRS 24-21-519[4]). Notaries should never surrender control of their journals to anyone, unless expressly subpoenaed by a court order. Even when an employer has paid for the Notary's official journal, it goes with the Notary upon termination of employment.

Lost Journal. If the Notary's journal is lost or stolen, the Notary must notify the Secretary of State within 30 days (CRS 24-21-519[8]). ■

Notary Certificate and Stamp

Notary Certificate

Requirement. In notarizing any document, a Notary must complete a Notary certificate at the time of notarization. The certificate is wording that indicates exactly what the Notary has certified. The Notary certificate wording may appear on the document itself or on an attachment to it. The certificate must (CRS 24-21-515[1]):

1. Be executed contemporaneously with the performance of the notarial act;

2. Be signed and dated by the Notary and be signed in the same manner as on file with the secretary of state;

3. Identify the county and state in which the notarial act is performed;

4. Contain the title "Notary Public"; and

5. Indicate the date of expiration of the Notary's commission.

Tangible Records. If a notarial act regarding a tangible (paper) document is performed, an official stamp must be affixed to the certificate.

Electronic Records. If a notarial act regarding an electronic record is performed, an official stamp must be attached to or logically associated with the certificate

Completing the Certificate. When filling in the blanks in the Notary certificate, Notaries should either type or print neatly in dark ink.

It is not necessary to select or cross out variable terms such as "he/she/they," "is/are" or a plural "(s)."

Correcting a Certificate. When filling out the certificate, the Notary needs to make sure any preprinted information is accurate. For example, the venue — the state and county in which the notarial act is taking place — may have been filled in prior to the notarization. If the preprinted venue is incorrect, the Notary must line through the incorrect state and/or county, write in the proper site of the notarization, and initial and date the change.

When correcting a Notary certificate the Notary must draw a line through the mistake with ink, write the correction above or beside it, then initial and date the correction (SOS website FAQ's).

Certificate Forms. When certificate wording is not preprinted on the document, or when preprinted wording is not acceptable, the Notary may attach a certificate form. This form typically is stapled to the document's left margin following the signature page.

If the certificate form is replacing unacceptable preprinted wording, the Notary should line through the preprinted wording and write below it, "See attached certificate." If the document has no preprinted wording, however, the Notary should not add this notation. Those words could be viewed as an unauthorized change to the document.

To prevent a certificate form from being removed and fraudulently placed on another document, the Notary may add a brief description of the document to the certificate: "This certificate is attached to a _____ (title or type of document), dated _____ (date), of _____ (number) pages, signed by _____ (name[s] of signer[s])."

The National Notary Association offers certificate forms that have similar wording preprinted on them; otherwise, the Notary will have to print, type, or stamp this information on each certificate form used. Finally, when Notaries attach a certificate form to a document, they always should note in their journals that they did so, as well as the means by which they attached the certificate to the document: "Certificate form stapled to document, following signature page."

While fraud-deterrent steps such as these can make it much more difficult for a certificate form to be removed and misused, there is no absolute protection against its removal and misuse. While a certificate form remains in their control, however, Notaries must absolutely ensure that it is attached only to its intended document.

Do Not Select Certificates. Nonattorney Notaries should never select Notary certificates for any transaction. It is not the role of a nonattorney Notary to decide what type of certificate — and thus what type of notarization — a document needs. As ministerial officials, Notaries generally follow instructions and complete forms that have been provided for them; they do not issue instructions and decide which forms are appropriate in a given case.

If a document is presented to a Notary without certificate wording and the signer does not know what type of notarization is appropriate, the signer should be asked to find out what kind of notarization and certificate are needed. Usually the agency that issued or will be accepting the document can provide this information. A Notary who selects certificates may be engaging in the unauthorized practice of law.

Do Not Pre-Sign or Pre-Stamp Certificates. A Notary must never sign and/or stamp certificates ahead of time or permit other persons to attach Notary certificate forms to documents.

A Notary must never give or mail unattached, signed, and stamped certificate forms to another person and trust that person to attach it to a particular document, even if asked to do so by a signer who previously appeared before the Notary.

These actions could facilitate fraud or forgery and, since such actions would be indefensible in a civil court of law, they could subject the Notary to lawsuits to recover damages resulting from the Notary's neglect or misconduct.

Notary Stamp

Requirement. Colorado Notaries are required to possess an official rubber stamp seal of office and use it on every document notarized (CRS 24-21-517).

Embossing Seal. Colorado Notaries are not permitted to provide, keep or use a seal embosser (CRS 24-21-517[2]).

Format and Required Information. Notary stamps must be rectangular and contain the following elements within the outline of the stamp:

- The Notary's name, as it appears on the Notary's certificate of commission;
- The Notary's identification number;
- The Notary's commission expiration date;
- The words "state of Colorado"; and
- The words "Notary Public".

Curative Seal Provision. A Notary stamp affixed to an instrument relating to real property that is not in compliance with Colorado law does not render the instrument or the notarization invalid or ineffective, nor does it render a real property title unmarketable.

Placement of Stamp Imprint. The Notary's official stamp imprint must be clear, legible and stamped by the Notary under or near the Notary's signature on the Notary certificate (Secretary of State handbook).

The Notary should not affix the stamp over any text on the document or certificate, especially if legibility is impaired. Some recorders will reject documents if writing or document text intrudes within the borders of the Notary's stamp.

If there is no room for a stamp, the Notary may have no choice but to complete and attach a certificate form that duplicates the Notary wording on the document.

L.S. On many certificates the letters "L.S." appear, indicating where the stamp is to be located. These letters abbreviate the Latin term *locus sigilli,* meaning "place of seal." The stamp impression should be affixed near but not over the letters, so that wording imprinted by the stamp will not be obscured.

Illegible Stamp. If an initial stamp imprint is unreadable and there is ample room on the document, another imprint can be affixed nearby. The illegibility of the first imprint will indicate why a second stamp imprint was necessary. The Notary should then record in the journal that a second impression was applied. A Notary should never attempt to fix an imperfect stamp imprint with pen, ink or correction fluid. This may be viewed as evidence of tampering and cause the document to be rejected by a receiving agency.

Electronic Signature in Lieu of Stamp. If a Notary notarizes an electronic document or record using the Notary's electronic signature, no physical stamp is necessary. Provided that all other conditions for notarizing electronically are met, the information contained in the Notary's electronic signature meets the statutory requirement. (See "Electronic Notarizations," pages 44–45.)

Personal Property. The Notary is responsible for the security of the stamp and may not allow anyone else to use the stamp (CRS 24-21-518[1]).

Lost Stamp. If a Notary's stamp is lost or stolen, the Notary or the Notary's personal representative or guardian must notify the Secretary of State in writing within 30 days (CRS 24-21-518[2]). ■

Electronic and Remote Online Notarizations

ELECTRONIC NOTARIZATION

Colorado law defines an electronic notarization as a notarization of electronic documents that includes the Notary's and the document signer's electronic signatures (8 CCR 1505-11, Rule 1.5).

Notification and Registration. Before performing an electronic notarization, a Notary must notify the secretary of state on an approved form and identify the technology the Notary intends to use. If the secretary of state has established standards for approval of technology, the technology must conform to the standards. A Notary may only electronically notarize a document after he or she has been approved by the secretary of state (CRS 24-21-520[b]; (8 CCR 1505-11, Rule 2.2.1).

Procedure. When performing an electronic notarization the signer must be in the physical presence of the Notary at the time of notarization. The Notary then identifies the signer based on personal knowledge or satisfactory evidence (see page 9) and completes the notarization using approved tamper-evident technology. Just like with paper notarizations, a journal entry is required.

Notary's Electronic Signature. The electronic signature of a Notary must contain or be accompanied by the following elements (CRS 24-21-520[3]):

1. Notary's name, as it appears on the notary's certificate of commission;

2. Notary's identification number;

3. The words "notary public" and "state of Colorado";

4. A document authentication number issued by the secretary of state; and

5. The words "my commission expires" followed by the expiration date of the notary's commission.

Document Authentication Number (DAN). In order to perform an electronic notarization, a notary must attach to the document a document authentication number (DAN), which is a unique document authentication number issued by the Secretary of State (CRS 12-55-112[4.5][b]).

A Notary may choose to either use a DAN as the Notary's electronic signature or adopt a different electronic signature which the Notary must always use in conjunction with a DAN (8 CCR 1505-11, Rule 2.2.1).

A Notary must (8 CCR 1505-11, Rule 2.2.2):

- Use a different DAN for each electronic notarization;

- Take reasonable measures to secure assigned DANs against another person's access or use and must not permit such access or use; and

- Request new DANs to replace lost or stolen DANs after notifying the Secretary in the same manner as for a journal or seal.

REMOTE ONLINE NOTARIZATION

Remote Online Notarization Defined

Effective December 31, 2020, approved Notaries in Colorado may perform Remote Online Notarizations. Remote Online Notarization, also referred to as RON, may be performed when the Notary and signer cannot meet face-to-face in the same room. RON requires the Notary and signer to meet via audio-video technology that allows them to see and hear each other in real-time (CRS 24-21-506). The electronic record or document and the electronic notary certificate are uploaded to a shared platform by a remote notarization system, and the notarization takes place via that platform. The Notary would still follow the fundamental steps for the notarization. The Notary screens the signer for identity, willingness and awareness and certifies the facts for the requested notarization. Then the Notary completes the electronic certificate and affixes an electronic signature and stamp. In addition to creating a journal record for the transaction, an audio-video recording of the transaction is required.

Authorization to Perform RON

For a Notary to be authorized to perform remote online notarial acts, the Notary must (CRS 24-21-514.5(3)):

- Notify the Secretary of State of their intention to perform RON
- Identify the RON technology systems the Notary will use
- Provide the notice in the following format:
    a. Include an affirmation that the Notary has read and will comply with any rules adopted by the state.
    b. Provide proof that the Notary has successfully completed any training and exam required by the state.

Location of Notary and Signer

The Notary must be located within the state of Colorado at the time of the remote online notarization and must identify the venue for the notarization as the jurisdiction within the state of Colorado where the Notary is located. However, the signer is not required to be located in Colorado at the time of notarization. The signer can be located in the state of Colorado, outside of Colorado but within the Unites States, or outside the United States. If the remotely located signer is outside of the United States (CRS 24-21-514.5(2)):

A) The Notary must have no actual knowledge that the notarial act is prohibited in the jurisdiction in which the signer is physically located at the time of notarization.

B) The remotely located signer must confirm to the Notary that the requested notarial act and the record relate to: a matter that will be filed with or is currently before a governmental entity in the US; or is related to property located in the US; or the transaction is substantially connected to the US.

Audio-Video Communication Quality Considerations

The Notary must:

1. Execute the notarial act in single real-time session.

2. Confirm that the record that is signed, acknowledged, or otherwise presented for notarization is the same record notarized by the Notary.

3. Confirm that the quality of the audio-video is sufficient to make the determinations required for the notarial act.

Identification of the Remotely Located Signer

Verifying the signer's identity remains one of the most important roles of the Notary. A Notary must determine identity of the remotely located individual through personal knowledge or satisfactory evidence. Satisfactory evidence includes at least one of the following (CRS 24-21-514.5(6)):

a. The oath or affirmation of a credible witness who personally knows the signer, is personally known to the Notary, and is in the physical presence of either the signer or Notary at the time of the notarization.

b. The remote presentation of a valid government-issued ID with a signature and photograph, along with credential analysis of the ID. Credential analysis is a process or service using a third party to affirm the validity of an ID through the review of public or proprietary data sources.

c. In addition, one of the following must be implemented:

   i. A dynamic, knowledge-based authentication assessment by a trusted third party. "Dynamic, Knowledge-Based Authentication" means an identity assessment that is based on a set of questions formulated from public or private data sources for which the signer has not previously provided an answer and that meets the rules adopted by the state; or

   ii. A valid public key certificate, which is an electronic credential used by the signer to sign the record and which identifies the signer. The public key certificate must comply with rules adopted by the state; or

   iii. An identity verification by a trusted third party that complies with the rules adopted by the state.

RON Record-Keeping Requirements

Electronic Journal. A remote online Notary must keep, maintain and protect an electronic journal of all remote online notarizations performed (CRS 24-21-519). The electronic journal record should include the same information as a traditional journal.

Audio-Video Recording. In addition to the electronic journal, an audio-video recording of the entire remote online notarization must be made if (CRS 24-21-514.5(9)): (a) the Notary first discloses to the remotely located individual the fact of the recording and the details of its intended storage, including where and for how long it will be stored; (b) the remotely located individual explicitly consents to both the recording and storage of the recording; and (c) the recording is stored in compliance with rules adopted by the Secretary of State. The Notary must also clarify that the recording of the remote notarization is in addition to a journal entry for the remote notarization.

At the commencement of the recording, the Notary must recite the following information: (a) the name of the Notary, (b) the date and time of the notarial act, (c) a description of the nature of the document or documents to which the notarial act is to relate, and (d) the identity of the remotely located individual whose signature is to be the subject of the notarial act and of any person who will act as a credible witness to identify the individual signer, and the method or methods by which the remotely located individual and any credible witness will be identified to the Notary.

The recording must also include:

- a declaration by the remotely located individual that the individual's signature on the record is knowingly and voluntarily made.

- an explanation by the Notary as to how the Notary knows the remotely located individual and how long the Notary has known the remotely located individual, if the remotely located individual is identified to the Notary by the Notary's personal knowledge.

- a statement by the Notary as to how the Notary knows the credible witness and how long the Notary has known the credible witness; and an explanation by the credible witness as to how the credible witness knows the remotely located individual and how long the credible witness has known the remotely located individual, if the remotely located individual is identified to the Notary by a credible witness.

- the statements, acts, and conduct necessary to perform the requested notarial act or supervision of signing or witnessing of the subject record.

The Notary must include the information listed above, as required under CRS 24-21-514.5(9)(b), but the Notary must make a good faith attempt not to include any other information.

Security of Journal and Recordings. The provisions of CRS 24-21-519 that pertain to the security, inspection, copying, and retention and disposition of a Notary's traditional journal also pertain to recordings of remote notarizations.

Certificate of Remote Notarial Act

As with traditional notarizations, the Notary must complete, sign and seal a Notary certificate for the transaction. When completing a Notary certificate for a remote online notarization, the certificate must indicate that the notarial act was performed using audio-video communication technology (CRS 24-21-515). The Notary will provide a tamper-evident electronic signature to the Notary certificate and will typically affix an electronic image of the Notary stamp.

Prohibited Documents

A Notary is prohibited from using a remote notarization system to notarize a record relating to the electoral process (CRS 24-21-514.5 [2][b][I]). ■

Misconduct, Fines and Penalties

Official Misconduct

First Degree Definition. A Notary commits first degree official misconduct if, while trying to obtain an illegal benefit or intentionally cause harm (CRS 18-8-404):

1. The Notary performs an unauthorized notarial act.
2. The Notary refuses to perform a law-required duty.
3. The Notary violates any law or rule relating to his or her notarial duties.

Class 2 Misdemeanor. First degree official misconduct is a class 2 misdemeanor (CRS 18-8-404).

Prohibited Acts

Notarizing After Commission Expiration. Colorado Notaries are prohibited from notarizing after the expiration of their commission. There is no grace period. Notarization after a commission has expired is a class 2 misdemeanor (CRS 24-21-523[1][k]).

Impersonation of Notary. A person who willfully impersonates a Notary while not being commissioned commits a class 2 misdemeanor (CRS 24-21-532).

Preparing Documents. Notaries may neither assist anyone in preparing a document nor fill in the blanks on a document, other than the Notary certificate (CRS 24-21-525[1][a]).

Claiming to Be Immigration Expert. A nonattorney Notary may not represent himself or herself to be an immigration expert unless he or she is designated by the U.S. Citizenship and Immigration Services or by the Board of Immigration Appeals (CRS 24-21-525[2][b]) and U.S. Penal Code Section 75 and U.S. Code Title 18, Section 137.

Notarizing Own Signature. A Notary may not notarize his or her own signature (CRS 24-21-504[b]).

Notarizing Without Signer Personally Appearing. A Notary may not notarize a signature without a signer physically appearing before the Notary (CRS 24-21-506).

Notarizing Without Verifying Signer's Identity. A Notary may not notarize any document without identifying the signer, either through personal knowledge, a credible identifying witness or acceptable ID cards (CRS 24-21-507).

Wrongful Possession. Any person who unlawfully possesses or uses a Notary's journal, stamp, electronic signature, or any papers, copies, or electronic records related to notarial acts commits a class 3 misdemeanor (CRS 24-21-533).

Effective March 1, 2022 Senate Bill 21-271 reclassifies the following criminal offenses:

1. A Notary who administers any oath knowing it to be false, or who knowingly makes a false certificate regarding an election matter for a municipal election, commits a class 2 misdemeanor, and not a misdemeanor, which is the penalty under current law.

2. A Notary who administers any oath knowing it to be false, or who knowingly makes a false certificate regarding a general, primary, recall, and congressional vacancy election matter, commits a class 2 misdemeanor, and not a misdemeanor, which is the penalty under current law.

3. A Notary who knowingly and willfully violates the Revised Uniform Law on Notarial Acts commits official misconduct and is guilty of a petty offense and not a class 2 misdemeanor, which is the penalty under current law, and is punishable upon conviction by a fine of up to $300, imprisonment for up to 10 days in county jail, or both.

4. Acting as or impersonating a Notary willfully while not lawfully commissioned to perform notarial acts is a petty offense and not a class 2 misdemeanor, which is the penalty under current law, and is punishable upon conviction by a fine of up to $300, imprisonment for up to 10 days in county jail, or both.

5. Anyone who unlawfully possesses and uses a Notary's journal, seal, electronic signature, or any papers, copies, or electronic records related to notarial acts commits a petty offense and not a class 3 misdemeanor, which is the penalty under current law, and is punishable upon conviction by a fine of up to $300, imprisonment for up to 10 days in county jail, or both.

Refusal or Revocation of Appointment

Secretary's Right to Investigate. The Secretary of State may investigate any accusation of wrongdoing that the Secretary believes is a violation of Colorado's Notary laws. An investigation may also begin upon reception of a signed complaint from any person (CRS 24-21-523[2]).

Notarize After Commission Expiration. The Colorado Secretary of State or Secretary's designee may suspend, deny or revoke the appointment of any Notary or applicant who knowingly acts as a Notary after his or her commission expires (CRS 24-21-523[1][k]).

Notarize When Commission Is Suspended. The Secretary of State or Secretary's designee may deny or take disciplinary action against the appointment of a Notary who fails to comply with any term of suspension imposed against the commission of a Notary or performs a notarial act when the commission is suspended (CRS 24-21-523[j]).

Failure of Duty. The Secretary of State or Secretary's designee may suspend or may revoke the appointment of any Notary who fails to perform the duties of a Notary Public. For example, a Notary who certifies an affidavit without administering the proper oath or affirmation may have the commission revoked (CRS 24-21-523[a]).

Overcharging. Although not specifically mentioned by law, a Notary who charges more than the maximum fees permitted by law could be failing to perform a duty of the office. Upon conviction, the Notary may face revocation of the commission.

Application Misstatement or Omission. A Notary who submits an application with substantial errors and/or omissions of fact may have his or her application denied or the commission suspended or revoked (CRS 24-21-523[b]).

Felony Conviction. A Notary who has been convicted of a felony may have the application denied or the commission suspended or revoked (CRS 24-21-523[c]).

Misdemeanor Involving Dishonesty means a violation of, or a conspiracy to violate, a civil or criminal law involving fraud, dishonesty, bribery, perjury, larceny, theft, robbery, extortion, forgery, counterfeiting, embezzlement, misappropriation of property, or any other offense adversely affecting a person's fitness to serve as a Notary Public. If a Notary has been convicted for a misdemeanor involving dishonesty within the last five years, the Notary's commission may be revoked or suspended (CRS 24-21-523[c]).

False Advertising. Notaries may not misleadingly advertise or represent that they have duties, rights or privileges that Notaries do not have (CRS 24-21-523[f]).

Advertising as Immigration Consultant. A nonattorney Notary who represents himself or herself as an immigration specialist or expert on immigration matters may have the commission revoked or suspended (CRS 24-21-523[f]).

Unauthorized Practice of Law. Any Notary found by any court to have engaged in the unauthorized practice of law commits a deceptive trade practice and may have the application denied or the commission revoked by the Secretary of State.

Specifically, the nonattorney Notary may not (CRS 24-21-525[2][a-d]):

- Assist in drafting legal documents, give legal advice, or otherwise practice law.
- Act as an immigration consultant or an expert on immigration matters.
- Represent a person in a judicial or administrative proceeding relating to immigration, or related matters.
- Receive compensation for drafting documents, representing a person in judicial or administrative proceedings, including matters related to immigration.
- Use the terms *Notario Publico* or *Notario* in any advertisement.

Notarizing a Blank Document. A Notary who notarizes a document with blank spaces on it may have the application denied or the commission suspended or revoked (CRS 24-21-525[7]).

Penalty for Commission Revocation. A Notary who has his or her commission revoked is permanently ineligible from holding another Colorado Notary commission (CRS 24-21-523[6]).

Disciplinary and Nondisciplinary Actions

Disciplinary Actions. The Secretary of State may revoke the commission of a Notary or suspend the commission of a Notary for a definite period of time (CRS 24-21-523).

Nondisciplinary Actions. The Secretary of State may issue a letter of admonition against the commission of a Notary, which may be placed in the Notary's file. A letter of admonition may be issued when the Secretary or Secretary's designee finds the Notary has committed misconduct in response to a complaint or investigation that does not warrant disciplinary action (CRS 24-21-523[4]).

Right to a Hearing

Revocation or Denial of Appointment. A Notary who has a commission revoked or whose application for appointment is denied may request an administrative hearing (CRS 24-21-523[3]).

Process. Once a Notary requests a hearing, it must be held speedily. The hearing may be held before either the Secretary of State or the Deputy Secretary of State (CRS 24-4-105).

Appeal. If the Secretary or Deputy Secretary of State rules against the Notary, the Notary has 20 days to appeal to the courts. The Notary or any other person may file papers on the Notary's behalf within 30 days after the original finding. The new hearing will be held before the appropriate judge. The appeal decision will be based solely upon the previous decision, the rulings on the proposed findings and conclusions, and any other exceptions or briefs filed (CRS 24-4-105).

Civil Lawsuit

Liability. As a ministerial official, a Colorado Notary is liable for all damages caused by any intentional or unintentional misconduct or neglect. A civil lawsuit against the Notary may seek financial recovery against any and all of the Notary's personal assets. ■

Colorado Laws Pertaining to Notaries Public

Reprinted on the following pages are the pertinent sections of the Colorado Revised Statutes (CRS) affecting Notaries and notarial acts. These statutes, along with this *Primer*, should be studied thoroughly before executing any notarial acts.

COLORADO REVISED STATUTES
TITLE 24
GOVERNMENT - STATE
STATE OFFICERS
ARTICLE 21
SECRETARY OF STATE - DEPARTMENT OF STATE

Part 5 - Revised Uniform Law on Notarial Acts

24-21-501. Short title. THE SHORT TITLE OF THIS PART 5 IS THE "REVISED UNIFORM LAW ON NOTARIAL ACTS".

24-21-502. Definitions. IN THIS PART 5:

(1) "ACKNOWLEDGMENT" MEANS A DECLARATION BY AN INDIVIDUAL BEFORE A NOTARIAL OFFICER THAT THE INDIVIDUAL HAS SIGNED A RECORD FOR THE PURPOSE STATED IN THE RECORD AND, IF THE RECORD IS SIGNED IN A REPRESENTATIVE CAPACITY, THAT THE INDIVIDUAL SIGNED THE RECORD WITH PROPER AUTHORITY AND SIGNED IT AS THE ACT OF THE INDIVIDUAL OR

ENTITY IDENTIFIED IN THE RECORD.

(2) "ELECTRONIC" MEANS RELATING TO TECHNOLOGY HAVING ELECTRICAL, DIGITAL, MAGNETIC, WIRELESS, OPTICAL, ELECTROMAGNETIC, OR SIMILAR CAPABILITIES.

(3) "ELECTRONIC RECORD" MEANS A RECORD CONTAINING INFORMATION THAT IS CREATED, GENERATED, SENT, COMMUNICATED, RECEIVED, OR STORED BY ELECTRONIC MEANS.

(4) "ELECTRONIC SIGNATURE" MEANS AN ELECTRONIC SYMBOL, SOUND, OR PROCESS ATTACHED TO OR LOGICALLY ASSOCIATED WITH AN ELECTRONIC RECORD AND EXECUTED OR ADOPTED BY AN INDIVIDUAL WITH THE INTENT TO SIGN THE ELECTRONIC RECORD.

(5) "IN A REPRESENTATIVE CAPACITY" MEANS ACTING AS:

(a) AN AUTHORIZED OFFICER, AGENT, PARTNER, TRUSTEE, OR OTHER REPRESENTATIVE FOR A PERSON OTHER THAN AN INDIVIDUAL;

(b) A PUBLIC OFFICER, PERSONAL REPRESENTATIVE, GUARDIAN, OR OTHER REPRESENTATIVE, IN THE CAPACITY STATED IN A RECORD;

(c) AN AGENT OR ATTORNEY-IN-FACT FOR A PRINCIPAL; OR

(d) AN AUTHORIZED REPRESENTATIVE OF ANOTHER IN ANY OTHER CAPACITY.

(6) "NOTARIAL ACT" MEANS AN ACT, WHETHER PERFORMED WITH RESPECT TO A TANGIBLE OR ELECTRONIC RECORD, THAT A NOTARIAL OFFICER MAY PERFORM UNDER THE LAW OF THIS STATE. THE TERM INCLUDES TAKING AN ACKNOWLEDGMENT, ADMINISTERING AN OATH OR AFFIRMATION, TAKING A DEPOSITION OR OTHER SWORN TESTIMONY, TAKING A VERIFICATION ON OATH OR AFFIRMATION, WITNESSING OR ATTESTING A SIGNATURE, CERTIFYING A COPY, AND NOTING A PROTEST OF A NEGOTIABLE INSTRUMENT.

(7) "NOTARIAL OFFICER" MEANS A NOTARY PUBLIC OR OTHER INDIVIDUAL AUTHORIZED TO PERFORM A NOTARIAL ACT.

(8) "NOTARY PUBLIC" MEANS AN INDIVIDUAL COMMISSIONED TO PERFORM A NOTARIAL ACT BY THE SECRETARY OF STATE.

(9) "OFFICIAL STAMP" MEANS A PHYSICAL IMAGE AFFIXED TO A TANGIBLE RECORD OR AN ELECTRONIC IMAGE ATTACHED TO OR LOGICALLY ASSOCIATED WITH AN ELECTRONIC RECORD.

(10) "PERSON" MEANS AN INDIVIDUAL, CORPORATION, BUSINESS TRUST, STATUTORY TRUST, ESTATE, TRUST, PARTNERSHIP, LIMITED LIABILITY COMPANY, ASSOCIATION, JOINT VENTURE, PUBLIC CORPORATION, GOVERNMENT OR GOVERNMENTAL SUBDIVISION, AGENCY, OR INSTRUMENTALITY, OR ANY OTHER LEGAL OR COMMERCIAL ENTITY.

(11) "RECORD" MEANS INFORMATION THAT IS INSCRIBED ON A TANGIBLE MEDIUM OR THAT IS STORED IN AN ELECTRONIC OR OTHER MEDIUM AND IS RETRIEVABLE IN PERCEIVABLE FORM.

(12) "SIGN" MEANS, WITH PRESENT INTENT TO AUTHENTICATE OR ADOPT A RECORD:

(a) TO EXECUTE OR ADOPT A TANGIBLE SYMBOL; OR

(b) TO ATTACH TO OR LOGICALLY ASSOCIATE WITH THE RECORD AN ELECTRONIC SYMBOL, SOUND, OR PROCESS.

(13) "SIGNATURE" MEANS A TANGIBLE SYMBOL OR AN ELECTRONIC SIGNATURE THAT EVIDENCES THE SIGNING OF A RECORD.

(14) "STAMPING DEVICE" MEANS:

(a) A PHYSICAL DEVICE CAPABLE OF AFFIXING TO A TANGIBLE RECORD AN OFFICIAL STAMP; OR

(b) AN ELECTRONIC DEVICE OR PROCESS CAPABLE OF ATTACHING TO OR LOGICALLY ASSOCIATING WITH AN ELECTRONIC RECORD AN OFFICIAL STAMP.

(15) "STATE" MEANS A STATE OF THE UNITED STATES, THE DISTRICT OF COLUMBIA, PUERTO RICO, THE UNITED STATES VIRGIN ISLANDS, OR ANY TERRITORY OR INSULAR POSSESSION SUBJECT TO THE JURISDICTION OF THE UNITED STATES.

(16) "VERIFICATION ON OATH OR AFFIRMATION" MEANS A DECLARATION, MADE BY AN INDIVIDUAL ON OATH OR AFFIRMATION BEFORE A NOTARIAL OFFICER, THAT A STATEMENT IN A RECORD IS TRUE.

24-21-503. Applicability. THIS PARTS APPLIES TO A NOTARIAL ACT PERFORMED ON OR AFTER THE EFFECTIVE DATE OF THIS PART 5.

24-21-504. Authority to perform notarial act. (1) A NOTARIAL OFFICER MAY PERFORM A NOTARIAL ACT AUTHORIZED BY THIS PART 5 OR BY LAW OF THIS STATE OTHER THAN THIS PART 5.

(2) A NOTARIAL OFFICER SHALL NOT PERFORM A NOTARIAL ACT WITH RESPECT TO A RECORD IN WHICH THE OFFICER HAS A DISQUALIFYING INTEREST. FOR THE PURPOSES OF THIS SECTION, A NOTARIAL OFFICER HAS A DISQUALIFYING INTEREST IN A RECORD IF:

(a) THE OFFICER OR THE OFFICER'S SPOUSE, PARTNER IN A CIVIL UNION, ANCESTOR, DESCENDENT, OR SIBLING IS A PARTY TO OR IS NAMED IN THE RECORD THAT IS TO BE NOTARIZED; OR

(b) THE OFFICER OR THE OFFICER'S SPOUSE OR PARTNER IN A CIVIL UNION MAY RECEIVE DIRECTLY, AND AS A PROXIMATE RESULT OF THE NOTARIZATION, ANY ADVANTAGE, RIGHT, TITLE, INTEREST, CASH, OR PROPERTY EXCEEDING IN VALUE THE SUM OF ANY FEE PROPERLY RECEIVED IN ACCORDANCE WITH THIS PART 5.

(3) A NOTARIAL ACT PERFORMED IN VIOLATION OF THIS SECTION IS VOIDABLE.

24-21-505. Requirements for certain notarial acts. (1) A NOTARIAL OFFICER WHO TAKES AN ACKNOWLEDGMENT OF A RECORD SHALL DETERMINE, FROM PERSONAL KNOWLEDGE OR SATISFACTORY EVIDENCE OF THE IDENTITY OF THE INDIVIDUAL, THAT THE INDIVIDUAL APPEARING BEFORE THE OFFICER AND MAKING THE ACKNOWLEDGMENT HAS THE IDENTITY CLAIMED AND THAT THE SIGNATURE ON THE RECORD IS THE SIGNATURE OF THE INDIVIDUAL.

(2) A NOTARIAL OFFICER WHO TAKES A VERIFICATION OF A STATEMENT ON OATH OR AFFIRMATION SHALL DETERMINE, FROM PERSONAL KNOWLEDGE OR SATISFACTORY EVIDENCE OF THE IDENTITY OF THE INDIVIDUAL, THAT THE INDIVIDUAL APPEARING BEFORE THE OFFICER AND MAKING THE VERIFICATION HAS THE IDENTITY CLAIMED AND THAT THE SIGNATURE ON THE STATEMENT VERIFIED IS THE SIGNATURE OF THE INDIVIDUAL.

(3) A NOTARIAL OFFICER WHO WITNESSES OR ATTESTS TO A SIGNATURE SHALL DETERMINE, FROM PERSONAL KNOWLEDGE OR SATISFACTORY EVIDENCE OF THE IDENTITY OF THE INDIVIDUAL, THAT THE INDIVIDUAL APPEARING BEFORE THE OFFICER AND SIGNING THE RECORD HAS THE IDENTITY CLAIMED.

(4) (a) A NOTARIAL OFFICER WHO CERTIFIES A COPY OF A RECORD OR AN ITEM THAT WAS COPIED SHALL DETERMINE THAT THE COPY IS A FULL, TRUE, AND ACCURATE TRANSCRIPTION OR REPRODUCTION OF THE RECORD OR ITEM.

(b) A NOTARIAL OFFICER SHALL NOT CERTIFY A COPY OF A RECORD THAT CAN BE OBTAINED FROM ANY OF THE FOLLOWING OFFICES IN THIS STATE:

(I) A CLERK AND RECORDER OF PUBLIC DOCUMENTS;

(II) THE SECRETARY OF STATE;

(III) THE STATE ARCHIVES; OR

(IV) AN OFFICE OF VITAL RECORDS.

(c) A NOTARIAL OFFICER SHALL NOT CERTIFY A COPY OF A RECORD IF THE RECORD STATES ON ITS FACE THAT IT IS ILLEGAL TO COPY THE RECORD.

(5) (a) A NOTARIAL OFFICER WHO MAKES OR NOTES A PROTEST OF A NEGOTIABLE INSTRUMENT SHALL DETERMINE THE MATTERS SET FORTH IN SECTION 4-3-505 (b) OF THE "UNIFORM COMMERCIAL CODE".

(b) A NOTARY PUBLIC SHALL NOT MAKE OR NOTE A PROTEST OF A NEGOTIABLE INSTRUMENT UNLESS THE NOTARY IS AN EMPLOYEE OF A FINANCIAL INSTITUTION ACTING IN THE COURSE AND SCOPE OF THE NOTARY'S EMPLOYMENT WITH THE FINANCIAL INSTITUTION.

24-21-506. Personal appearance required. IF A NOTARIAL ACT RELATES TO A STATEMENT MADE IN OR A SIGNATURE EXECUTED ON A RECORD, THE INDIVIDUAL MAKING THE STATEMENT OR EXECUTING THE SIGNATURE SHALL APPEAR PERSONALLY BEFORE THE NOTARIAL OFFICER.

24-21-507. Identification of individual. (1) A NOTARIAL OFFICER HAS PERSONAL KNOWLEDGE OF THE IDENTITY OF AN INDIVIDUAL APPEARING BEFORE THE OFFICER IF THE INDIVIDUAL IS PERSONALLY KNOWN TO THE OFFICER THROUGH DEALINGS SUFFICIENT TO PROVIDE REASONABLE CERTAINTY THAT THE INDIVIDUAL HAS THE IDENTITY CLAIMED.

(2) A NOTARIAL OFFICER HAS SATISFACTORY EVIDENCE OF THE IDENTITY OF AN INDIVIDUAL APPEARING BEFORE THE OFFICER IF THE OFFICER CAN IDENTIFY THE INDIVIDUAL:

(a) BY MEANS OF:

(I) A PASSPORT, DRIVER'S LICENSE, OR GOVERNMENT-ISSUED NONDRIVER IDENTIFICATION CARD THAT IS CURRENT OR EXPIRED NOT MORE THAN ONE YEAR BEFORE PERFORMANCE OF THE NOTARIAL ACT; OR

(II) ANOTHER FORM OF GOVERNMENT IDENTIFICATION ISSUED TO THE INDIVIDUAL THAT IS CURRENT OR EXPIRED NOT MORE THAN ONE YEAR BEFORE PERFORMANCE OF THE NOTARIAL ACT, CONTAINS THE SIGNATURE OR A PHOTOGRAPH OF THE INDIVIDUAL, AND IS SATISFACTORY TO THE OFFICER; OR

(b) BY A VERIFICATION ON OATH OR AFFIRMATION OF A CREDIBLE WITNESS PERSONALLY APPEARING BEFORE THE OFFICER AND KNOWN TO THE OFFICER

OR WHOM THE OFFICER CAN IDENTIFY ON THE BASIS OF A PASSPORT, DRIVER'S LICENSE, OR GOVERNMENT-ISSUED NONDRIVER IDENTIFICATION CARD THAT IS CURRENT OR EXPIRED NOT MORE THAN ONE YEAR BEFORE PERFORMANCE OF THE NOTARIAL ACT.

(3) A NOTARIAL OFFICER MAY REQUIRE AN INDIVIDUAL TO PROVIDE ADDITIONAL INFORMATION OR IDENTIFICATION CREDENTIALS NECESSARY TO ASSURE THE OFFICER OF THE IDENTITY OF THE INDIVIDUAL.

24-21-508. Authority to refuse to perform notarial act. (1) A NOTARIAL OFFICER MAY REFUSE TO PERFORM A NOTARIAL ACT IF THE OFFICER IS NOT SATISFIED THAT:

(a) THE INDIVIDUAL EXECUTING THE RECORD IS COMPETENT OR HAS THE CAPACITY TO EXECUTE THE RECORD; OR

(b) THE INDIVIDUAL'S SIGNATURE IS KNOWINGLY AND VOLUNTARILY MADE.

(2) A NOTARIAL OFFICER MAY REFUSE TO PERFORM A NOTARIAL ACT UNLESS REFUSAL IS PROHIBITED BY LAW OTHER THAN THIS PART 5.

24-21-509. Signature if individual unable to sign. (1) IF AN INDIVIDUAL IS PHYSICALLY UNABLE TO SIGN A RECORD, THE INDIVIDUAL MAY, IN THE PRESENCE OF THE NOTARIAL OFFICER, DIRECT AN INDIVIDUAL OTHER THAN THE NOTARIAL OFFICER TO SIGN THE INDIVIDUAL'S NAME ON THE RECORD. THE NOTARIAL OFFICER SHALL INSERT "SIGNATURE AFFIXED BY (NAME OF OTHER INDIVIDUAL) AT THE DIRECTION OF (NAME OF INDIVIDUAL)" OR WORDS OF SIMILAR IMPORT UNDER OR NEAR THE SIGNATURE.

(2) A NOTARY PUBLIC MAY USE SIGNALS OR ELECTRONIC OR MECHANICAL MEANS TO TAKE AN ACKNOWLEDGMENT FROM, ADMINISTER AN OATH OR AFFIRMATION TO, OR OTHERWISE COMMUNICATE WITH ANY INDIVIDUAL IN THE PRESENCE OF THE NOTARY PUBLIC WHEN IT APPEARS THAT THE INDIVIDUAL IS UNABLE TO COMMUNICATE VERBALLY OR IN WRITING.

24-21-510. Notarial act in this state. (1) A NOTARIAL ACT MAY BE PERFORMED IN THIS STATE BY:

(a) A NOTARY PUBLIC OF THIS STATE;

(b) A JUDGE, CLERK, OR DEPUTY CLERK OF A COURT OF THIS STATE; OR

(c) ANY OTHER INDIVIDUAL AUTHORIZED TO PERFORM THE SPECIFIC ACT BY THE LAW OF THIS STATE.

(2) THE SIGNATURE AND TITLE OF AN INDIVIDUAL PERFORMING A NOTARIAL ACT IN THIS STATE ARE PRIMA FACIE EVIDENCE THAT THE SIGNATURE IS GENUINE AND THAT THE INDIVIDUAL HOLDS THE DESIGNATED TITLE.

(3) THE SIGNATURE AND TITLE OF A NOTARIAL OFFICER DESCRIBED IN SUBSECTION (1)(a) OR (1)(b) OF THIS SECTION CONCLUSIVELY ESTABLISH THE AUTHORITY OF THE OFFICER TO PERFORM THE NOTARIAL ACT.

24-21-511. Notarial act in another state. (1) A NOTARIAL ACT PERFORMED IN ANOTHER STATE HAS THE SAME EFFECT UNDER THE LAW OF THIS STATE AS IF PERFORMED BY A NOTARIAL OFFICER OF THIS STATE IF THE ACT PERFORMED IN THAT STATE IS PERFORMED BY:

(a) A NOTARY PUBLIC OF THAT STATE;

(b) A JUDGE, CLERK, OR DEPUTY CLERK OF A COURT OF THAT STATE; OR

(c) ANY OTHER INDIVIDUAL AUTHORIZED BY THE LAW OF THAT STATE TO PERFORM THE NOTARIAL ACT.

(2) THE SIGNATURE AND TITLE OF AN INDIVIDUAL PERFORMING A NOTARIAL ACT IN ANOTHER STATE ARE PRIMA FACIE EVIDENCE THAT THE SIGNATURE IS GENUINE AND THAT THE INDIVIDUAL HOLDS THE DESIGNATED TITLE.

(3) THE SIGNATURE AND TITLE OF A NOTARIAL OFFICER DESCRIBED IN SUBSECTION (1)(a) OR (1)(b) OF THIS SECTION CONCLUSIVELY ESTABLISH THE AUTHORITY OF THE OFFICER TO PERFORM THE NOTARIAL ACT.

24-21-512. Notarial act under authority of federally recognized Indian tribe. (1) A NOTARIAL ACT PERFORMED UNDER THE AUTHORITY AND IN THE JURISDICTION OF A FEDERALLY RECOGNIZED INDIAN TRIBE HAS THE SAME EFFECT AS IF PERFORMED BY A NOTARIAL OFFICER OF THIS STATE IF THE ACT PERFORMED IN THE JURISDICTION OF THE TRIBE IS PERFORMED BY:

(a) A NOTARY PUBLIC OF THE TRIBE;

(b) A JUDGE, CLERK, OR DEPUTY CLERK OF A COURT OF THE TRIBE; OR

(c) ANY OTHER INDIVIDUAL AUTHORIZED BY THE LAW OF THE TRIBE TO PERFORM THE NOTARIAL ACT.

(2) THE SIGNATURE AND TITLE OF AN INDIVIDUAL PERFORMING A NOTARIAL ACT UNDER THE AUTHORITY OF AND IN THE JURISDICTION OF A FEDERALLY RECOGNIZED INDIAN TRIBE ARE PRIMA FACIE EVIDENCE THAT THE SIGNATURE IS GENUINE AND THAT THE INDIVIDUAL HOLDS THE DESIGNATED TITLE.

(3) THE SIGNATURE AND TITLE OF A NOTARIAL OFFICER DESCRIBED IN SUBSECTION (1)(a) OR (1)(b) OF THIS SECTION CONCLUSIVELY ESTABLISH THE AUTHORITY OF THE OFFICER TO PERFORM THE NOTARIAL ACT.

24-21-513. Notarial act under federal authority. (1) A NOTARIAL ACT PERFORMED UNDER FEDERAL LAW HAS THE SAME EFFECT UNDER THE LAW OF THIS STATE AS IF PERFORMED BY A NOTARIAL OFFICER OF THIS STATE IF THE ACT PERFORMED UNDER FEDERAL LAW IS PERFORMED BY:

(a) A JUDGE, CLERK, OR DEPUTY CLERK OF A COURT;

(b) AN INDIVIDUAL IN MILITARY SERVICE OR PERFORMING DUTIES UNDER THE AUTHORITY OF MILITARY SERVICE WHO IS AUTHORIZED TO PERFORM NOTARIAL ACTS UNDER FEDERAL LAW;

(c) AN INDIVIDUAL DESIGNATED A NOTARIZING OFFICER BY THE UNITED STATES DEPARTMENT OF STATE FOR PERFORMING NOTARIAL ACTS OVERSEAS; OR

(d) ANY OTHER INDIVIDUAL AUTHORIZED BY FEDERAL LAW TO PERFORM THE NOTARIAL ACT.

(2) THE SIGNATURE AND TITLE OF AN INDIVIDUAL ACTING UNDER FEDERAL AUTHORITY AND PERFORMING A NOTARIAL ACT ARE PRIMA FACIE EVIDENCE THAT THE SIGNATURE IS GENUINE AND THAT THE INDIVIDUAL HOLDS THE DESIGNATED TITLE.

(3) THE SIGNATURE AND TITLE OF AN OFFICER DESCRIBED IN SUBSECTION (1) (a), (1)(b), OR (1)(c) OF THIS SECTION CONCLUSIVELY ESTABLISH THE AUTHORITY OF THE OFFICER TO PERFORM THE NOTARIAL ACT.

24-21-514. Foreign notarial act. (1) IN THIS SECTION, "FOREIGN STATE" MEANS A GOVERNMENT OTHER THAN THE UNITED STATES, A STATE, OR A FEDERALLY RECOGNIZED INDIAN TRIBE.

(2) IF A NOTARIAL ACT IS PERFORMED UNDER AUTHORITY AND IN THE JURISDICTION OF A FOREIGN STATE OR CONSTITUENT UNIT OF THE FOREIGN STATE OR IS PERFORMED UNDER THE AUTHORITY OF A MULTINATIONAL OR INTERNATIONAL GOVERNMENTAL ORGANIZATION, THE ACT HAS THE SAME EFFECT UNDER THE LAW OF THIS STATE AS IF PERFORMED BY A NOTARIAL OFFICER OF THIS STATE.

(3) IF THE TITLE OF OFFICE AND INDICATION OF AUTHORITY TO PERFORM NOTARIAL ACTS IN A FOREIGN STATE APPEARS IN A DIGEST OF FOREIGN LAW OR IN A LIST CUSTOMARILY USED AS A SOURCE FOR THAT INFORMATION, THE AUTHORITY OF AN OFFICER WITH THAT TITLE TO PERFORM NOTARIAL ACTS IS CONCLUSIVELY ESTABLISHED.

(4) THE SIGNATURE AND OFFICIAL STAMP OF AN INDIVIDUAL HOLDING AN OFFICE DESCRIBED IN SUBSECTION (3) OF THIS SECTION ARE PRIMA FACIE EVIDENCE THAT THE SIGNATURE IS GENUINE AND THE INDIVIDUAL HOLDS THE DESIGNATED TITLE.

(5) AN APOSTILLE IN THE FORM PRESCRIBED BY THE HAGUE CONVENTION OF OCTOBER 5, 1961, AND ISSUED BY A FOREIGN STATE PARTY TO THE CONVENTION CONCLUSIVELY ESTABLISHES THAT THE SIGNATURE OF THE NOTARIAL OFFICER IS GENUINE AND THAT THE OFFICER HOLDS THE INDICATED OFFICE.

(6) A CONSULAR AUTHENTICATION ISSUED BY AN INDIVIDUAL DESIGNATED BY THE UNITED STATES DEPARTMENT OF STATE AS A NOTARIZING OFFICER FOR PERFORMING NOTARIAL ACTS OVERSEAS AND ATTACHED TO THE RECORD WITH RESPECT TO WHICH THE NOTARIAL ACT IS PERFORMED CONCLUSIVELY ESTABLISHES THAT THE SIGNATURE OF THE NOTARIAL OFFICER IS GENUINE AND THAT THE OFFICER HOLDS THE INDICATED OFFICE.

24-21-515. Certificate of notarial act. (1) A NOTARIAL ACT MUST BE EVIDENCED BY A CERTIFICATE. THE CERTIFICATE MUST:

(a) BE EXECUTED CONTEMPORANEOUSLY WITH THE PERFORMANCE OF THE NOTARIAL ACT;

(b) BE SIGNED AND DATED BY THE NOTARIAL OFFICER AND, IF THE NOTARIAL OFFICER IS A NOTARY PUBLIC, BE SIGNED IN THE SAME MANNER AS ON FILE WITH THE SECRETARY OF STATE;

(c) IDENTIFY THE COUNTY AND STATE IN WHICH THE NOTARIAL ACT IS PERFORMED;

(d) CONTAIN THE TITLE OF OFFICE OF THE NOTARIAL OFFICER; AND

(e) IF THE NOTARIAL OFFICER IS A NOTARY PUBLIC, INDICATE THE DATE OF EXPIRATION OF THE OFFICER'S COMMISSION.

(2) IF A NOTARIAL ACT REGARDING A TANGIBLE RECORD IS PERFORMED BY A NOTARY PUBLIC, AN OFFICIAL STAMP MUST BE AFFIXED TO THE CERTIFICATE. IF A NOTARIAL ACT IS PERFORMED REGARDING A TANGIBLE RECORD BY A NOTARIAL OFFICER OTHER THAN A NOTARY PUBLIC AND THE CERTIFICATE CONTAINS THE INFORMATION SPECIFIED IN SUBSECTIONS (1)(b), (1)(c), AND (1)(d) OF THIS SECTION, AN OFFICIAL STAMP MAY BE AFFIXED TO THE CERTIFICATE. IF A NOTARIAL ACT REGARDING AN ELECTRONIC RECORD IS PERFORMED

BY A NOTARIAL OFFICER AND THE CERTIFICATE CONTAINS THE INFORMATION SPECIFIED IN SUBSECTIONS (1)(b), (1)(c), AND (1)(d) OF THIS SECTION, AN OFFICIAL STAMP MAY BE ATTACHED TO OR LOGICALLY ASSOCIATED WITH THE CERTIFICATE.

(3) A CERTIFICATE OF A NOTARIAL ACT IS SUFFICIENT IF IT MEETS THE REQUIREMENTS OF SUBSECTIONS (1) AND (2) OF THIS SECTION AND:

(a) IS IN A SHORT FORM SET FORTH IN SECTION 24-21-516;

(b) IS IN A FORM OTHERWISE PERMITTED BY THE LAW OF THIS STATE;

(c) IS IN A FORM PERMITTED BY THE LAW APPLICABLE IN THE JURISDICTION IN WHICH THE NOTARIAL ACT WAS PERFORMED; OR

(d) SETS FORTH THE ACTIONS OF THE NOTARIAL OFFICER AND THE ACTIONS ARE SUFFICIENT TO MEET THE REQUIREMENTS OF THE NOTARIAL ACT AS PROVIDED IN SECTIONS 24-21-505, 24-21-506, AND 24-21-507 OR LAW OF THIS STATE OTHER THAN THIS PART 5.

(4) BY EXECUTING A CERTIFICATE OF A NOTARIAL ACT, A NOTARIAL OFFICER CERTIFIES THAT THE OFFICER HAS COMPLIED WITH THE REQUIREMENTS AND MADE THE DETERMINATIONS SPECIFIED IN SECTIONS 24-21-504, 24-21-505, AND 24-21-506.

(5) A NOTARIAL OFFICER SHALL NOT AFFIX THE OFFICER'S SIGNATURE TO, OR LOGICALLY ASSOCIATE IT WITH, A CERTIFICATE UNTIL THE NOTARIAL ACT HAS BEEN PERFORMED.

(6) IF A NOTARIAL ACT IS PERFORMED REGARDING A TANGIBLE RECORD, A CERTIFICATE MUST BE PART OF, OR SECURELY ATTACHED TO, THE RECORD. IF A NOTARIAL ACT IS PERFORMED REGARDING AN ELECTRONIC RECORD, THE CERTIFICATE MUST BE AFFIXED TO, OR LOGICALLY ASSOCIATED WITH, THE ELECTRONIC RECORD. IF THE SECRETARY OF STATE HAS ESTABLISHED STANDARDS PURSUANT TO SECTION 24-21-527 FOR ATTACHING, AFFIXING, OR LOGICALLY ASSOCIATING THE CERTIFICATE, THE PROCESS MUST CONFORM TO THE STANDARDS.

24-21-516. Short form certificates. (1) THE FOLLOWING SHORT FORM CERTIFICATES OF NOTARIAL ACTS ARE SUFFICIENT FOR THE PURPOSES INDICATED, IF COMPLETED WITH THE INFORMATION REQUIRED BY SECTION 24-21-515 (1) AND (2):

(a) FOR AN ACKNOWLEDGMENT IN AN INDIVIDUAL CAPACITY:

STATE OF _____
COUNTY OF _____

THIS RECORD WAS ACKNOWLEDGED BEFORE ME ON _____
(DATE) BY _____ (NAME(S) OF INDIVIDUAL(S))

_____
SIGNATURE OF NOTARIAL OFFICER

STAMP

_____
((TITLE OF OFFICE))
MY COMMISSION EXPIRES _____:

(b) FOR AN ACKNOWLEDGMENT IN A REPRESENTATIVE CAPACITY:

    STATE OF _____
    COUNTY OF _____

    THIS RECORD WAS ACKNOWLEDGED BEFORE ME ON _____
    (DATE) BY _____(NAME(S) OF INDIVIDUAL(S))
    AS _____(TYPE OF AUTHORITY, SUCH AS OFFICER OR TRUSTEE)
    OF (NAME OF PARTY ON BEHALF OF WHOM RECORD WAS EXECUTED).

    _____
    SIGNATURE OF NOTARIAL OFFICER

    STAMP

    _____
    ((TITLE OF OFFICE))
    MY COMMISSION EXPIRES _____:

(c) FOR A VERIFICATION ON OATH OR AFFIRMATION:

    STATE OF _____
    COUNTY OF _____

    SIGNED AND SWORN TO (OR AFFIRMED) BEFORE ME ON _____(DATE) BY
    _____ (NAME(S) OF INDIVIDUAL(S) MAKING STATEMENT)

    _____
    SIGNATURE OF NOTARIAL OFFICER

    STAMP

    _____
    (TITLE OF OFFICE))
    MY COMMISSION EXPIRES: _____

(d) FOR WITNESSING OR ATTESTING A SIGNATURE:

    STATE OF _____
    COUNTY OF _____

    SIGNED BEFORE ME ON _____ (DATE) BY _____ (NAME(S) OF
    INDIVIDUAL(S))

    _____
    SIGNATURE OF NOTARIAL OFFICER

    STAMP

    _____
    (TITLE OF OFFICE)
    MY COMMISSION EXPIRES _____:

(e) FOR CERTIFYING A COPY OF A RECORD:

STATE OF _____
COUNTY OF _____

I CERTIFY THAT THIS IS A TRUE AND CORRECT COPY OF A RECORD IN THE POSSESSION OF _____
DATED _____

_____
SIGNATURE OF NOTARIAL OFFICER
(_____(TITLE OF OFFICE)_____)
MY COMMISSION EXPIRES _____:

24-21-517. Official stamp. (1) THE OFFICIAL STAMP OF A NOTARY PUBLIC MUST:

(a) BE RECTANGULAR AND CONTAIN ONLY THE OUTLINE OF THE SEAL AND THE FOLLOWING INFORMATION PRINTED WITHIN THE OUTLINE OF THE SEAL:

(I) THE NOTARY PUBLIC'S NAME, AS IT APPEARS ON THE NOTARY'S CERTIFICATE OF COMMISSION;

(II) THE NOTARY'S IDENTIFICATION NUMBER;

(III) THE NOTARY'S COMMISSION EXPIRATION DATE;

(IV) THE WORDS "STATE OF COLORADO"; AND

(V) THE WORDS "NOTARY PUBLIC"; AND

(b) BE CAPABLE OF BEING COPIED TOGETHER WITH THE RECORD TO WHICH IT IS AFFIXED OR ATTACHED OR WITH WHICH IT IS LOGICALLY ASSOCIATED.

(2) A NOTARY PUBLIC SHALL NOT PROVIDE, KEEP, OR USE A SEAL EMBOSSER.

24-21-518. Stamping device. (1) A NOTARY PUBLIC IS RESPONSIBLE FOR THE SECURITY OF THE NOTARY PUBLIC'S STAMPING DEVICE AND MAY NOT ALLOW ANOTHER INDIVIDUAL TO USE THE DEVICE TO PERFORM A NOTARIAL ACT. ON RESIGNATION FROM, OR THE REVOCATION OR EXPIRATION OF, THE NOTARY PUBLIC'S COMMISSION, OR ON THE EXPIRATION OF THE DATE SET FORTH IN THE STAMPING DEVICE, IF ANY, THE NOTARY PUBLIC SHALL DISABLE THE STAMPING DEVICE BY DESTROYING, DEFACING, DAMAGING, ERASING, OR SECURING IT AGAINST USE IN A MANNER THAT RENDERS IT UNUSABLE. ON THE DEATH OR ADJUDICATION OF INCOMPETENCY OF A NOTARY PUBLIC, THE NOTARY PUBLIC'S PERSONAL REPRESENTATIVE OR GUARDIAN OR ANY OTHER PERSON KNOWINGLY IN POSSESSION OF THE STAMPING DEVICE SHALL RENDER IT UNUSABLE BY DESTROYING, DEFACING, DAMAGING, ERASING, OR SECURING IT AGAINST USE IN A MANNER THAT RENDERS IT UNUSABLE.

(2) IF A NOTARY PUBLIC'S STAMPING DEVICE IS LOST OR STOLEN, THE NOTARY PUBLIC OR THE NOTARY PUBLIC'S PERSONAL REPRESENTATIVE OR GUARDIAN SHALL NOTIFY THE SECRETARY OF STATE IN WRITING WITHIN THIRTY DAYS AFTER DISCOVERING THAT THE DEVICE IS LOST OR STOLEN.

24-21-519. Journal. (1) A NOTARY PUBLIC SHALL MAINTAIN A JOURNAL IN WHICH THE NOTARY PUBLIC CHRONICLES ALL NOTARIAL ACTS THAT THE NOTARY PUBLIC PERFORMS. THE NOTARY PUBLIC SHALL RETAIN THE JOURNAL FOR

TEN YEARS AFTER THE PERFORMANCE OF THE LAST NOTARIAL ACT CHRONICLED IN THE JOURNAL.

(2) A JOURNAL MAY BE CREATED ON A TANGIBLE MEDIUM OR IN AN ELECTRONIC FORMAT. IF A JOURNAL IS MAINTAINED ON A TANGIBLE MEDIUM, IT MUST BE A PERMANENT, BOUND REGISTER WITH NUMBERED PAGES. IF A JOURNAL IS MAINTAINED IN AN ELECTRONIC FORMAT, IT MUST BE IN A PERMANENT, TAMPER-EVIDENT ELECTRONIC FORMAT COMPLYING WITH THE RULES OF THE SECRETARY OF STATE.

(3) AN ENTRY IN A JOURNAL MUST BE MADE CONTEMPORANEOUSLY WITH PERFORMANCE OF THE NOTARIAL ACT AND CONTAIN THE FOLLOWING INFORMATION:

(a) THE DATE AND TIME OF THE NOTARIAL ACT;

(b) A DESCRIPTION OF THE RECORD, IF ANY, AND TYPE OF NOTARIAL ACT;

(c) THE FULL NAME AND ADDRESS OF EACH INDIVIDUAL FOR WHOM THE NOTARIAL ACT IS PERFORMED;

(d) THE SIGNATURE OR ELECTRONIC SIGNATURE OF EACH INDIVIDUAL FOR WHOM THE NOTARIAL ACT IS PERFORMED;

(e) IF IDENTITY OF THE INDIVIDUAL IS BASED ON PERSONAL KNOWLEDGE, A STATEMENT TO THAT EFFECT;

(f) IF IDENTITY OF THE INDIVIDUAL IS BASED ON SATISFACTORY EVIDENCE, A BRIEF DESCRIPTION OF THE METHOD OF IDENTIFICATION AND THE TYPE OF IDENTIFICATION CREDENTIAL PRESENTED, IF ANY; AND

(g) THE FEE, IF ANY, CHARGED BY THE NOTARY PUBLIC.

(4) A NOTARY PUBLIC IS RESPONSIBLE FOR THE SECURITY OF THE NOTARY PUBLIC'S JOURNAL. A NOTARY PUBLIC SHALL KEEP THE JOURNAL IN A SECURE AREA UNDER THE EXCLUSIVE CONTROL OF THE NOTARY, AND SHALL NOT ALLOW ANY OTHER NOTARY TO USE THE JOURNAL.

(5) UPON WRITTEN REQUEST OF ANY MEMBER OF THE PUBLIC, WHICH REQUEST MUST INCLUDE THE NAME OF THE PARTIES, THE TYPE OF DOCUMENT, AND THE MONTH AND YEAR IN WHICH A RECORD WAS NOTARIZED, A NOTARY PUBLIC MAY SUPPLY A CERTIFIED COPY OF THE LINE ITEM REPRESENTING THE REQUESTED TRANSACTION. A NOTARY PUBLIC MAY CHARGE THE FEE ALLOWED IN SECTION 24-21-529 FOR EACH CERTIFIED COPY OF A LINE ITEM, AND SHALL RECORD THE TRANSACTION IN THE NOTARY'S JOURNAL.

(6) THE SECRETARY OF STATE MAY AUDIT OR INSPECT A NOTARY PUBLIC'S JOURNAL WITHOUT RESTRICTION. A NOTARY PUBLIC SHALL SURRENDER THE NOTARY'S JOURNAL TO THE SECRETARY OF STATE UPON RECEIVING A WRITTEN REQUEST.

(7) A CERTIFIED PEACE OFFICER, AS DEFINED IN SECTION 16-2.5-102, ACTING IN THE COURSE OF AN OFFICIAL INVESTIGATION MAY INSPECT A NOTARY PUBLIC'S JOURNAL WITHOUT RESTRICTION.

(8) IF A NOTARY PUBLIC'S JOURNAL IS LOST OR STOLEN, THE NOTARY PUBLIC SHALL NOTIFY THE SECRETARY OF STATE IN WRITING WITHIN THIRTY DAYS AFTER DISCOVERING THAT THE JOURNAL IS LOST OR STOLEN.

(9) ON RESIGNATION FROM, OR THE REVOCATION OR EXPIRATION OF, A NOTARY PUBLIC'S COMMISSION, THE NOTARY PUBLIC SHALL RETAIN THE NOTARY PUBLIC'S JOURNAL IN ACCORDANCE WITH SUBSECTION (1) OF THIS SECTION AND INFORM THE SECRETARY OF STATE WHERE THE JOURNAL IS LOCATED.

(10) (a) INSTEAD OF RETAINING A JOURNAL AS PROVIDED IN SUBSECTIONS (1) AND (9) OF THIS SECTION, A CURRENT OR FORMER NOTARY PUBLIC MAY:

(I) TRANSMIT THE JOURNAL TO THE STATE ARCHIVES ESTABLISHED PURSUANT TO PART 1 OF ARTICLE 80 OF THIS TITLE 24; OR (II) LEAVE THE JOURNAL WITH THE NOTARY'S FIRM OR EMPLOYER IN THE REGULAR COURSE OF BUSINESS.

(b) IF NOTARY PUBLIC ACTS PURSUANT TO SUBSECTION (10)(a) OF THIS SECTION, THE NOTARY PUBLIC IS NO LONGER SUBJECT TO SUBSECTION (5) OF THIS SECTION AND SHALL NOTIFY THE SECRETARY OF STATE IN WRITING WHETHER THE NOTARY HAS TRANSMITTED THE JOURNAL TO THE STATE ARCHIVES OR THE FIRM OR EMPLOYER, INCLUDING THE CONTACT INFORMATION FOR THE FIRM OR EMPLOYER IF THE NOTARY LEAVES THE JOURNAL WITH THE NOTARY'S FIRM OR EMPLOYER.

(c) INSTEAD OF MAINTAINING A JOURNAL AS REQUIRED BY SUBSECTION (1) OF THIS SECTION, A NOTARY PUBLIC MAY MAINTAIN THE ORIGINAL OR A COPY, INCLUDING AN ELECTRONIC RECORD, OF A DOCUMENT THAT CONTAINS THE INFORMATION OTHERWISE REQUIRED TO BE ENTERED IN THE NOTARY'S JOURNAL IF THE NOTARY'S FIRM OR EMPLOYER RETAINS THE ORIGINAL, COPY, OR ELECTRONIC RECORD IN THE REGULAR COURSE OF BUSINESS.

(11) ON THE DEATH OR ADJUDICATION OF INCOMPETENCY OF A CURRENT OR FORMER NOTARY PUBLIC, THE NOTARY PUBLIC'S PERSONAL REPRESENTATIVE OR GUARDIAN OR ANY OTHER PERSON KNOWINGLY IN POSSESSION OF THE JOURNAL SHALL TRANSMIT IT TO THE STATE ARCHIVES ESTABLISHED PURSUANT TO PART 1 OF ARTICLE 80 OF THIS TITLE 24. THE PERSON SHALL NOTIFY THE SECRETARY OF STATE IN WRITING WHEN THE PERSON TRANSMITS THE JOURNAL TO THE STATE ARCHIVES.

24-21-520. Notification regarding performance of notarial act on electronic record - selection of technology. (1) A NOTARY PUBLIC MAY SELECT ONE OR MORE TAMPER-EVIDENT TECHNOLOGIES TO PERFORM NOTARIAL ACTS WITH RESPECT TO ELECTRONIC RECORDS. A PERSON MAY NOT REQUIRE A NOTARY PUBLIC TO PERFORM A NOTARIAL ACT WITH RESPECT TO AN ELECTRONIC RECORD WITH A TECHNOLOGY THAT THE NOTARY PUBLIC HAS NOT SELECTED.

(2) BEFORE A NOTARY PUBLIC PERFORMS THE NOTARY PUBLIC'S INITIAL NOTARIAL ACT WITH RESPECT TO AN ELECTRONIC RECORD, A NOTARY PUBLIC SHALL NOTIFY THE SECRETARY OF STATE THAT THE NOTARY PUBLIC WILL BE PERFORMING NOTARIAL ACTS WITH RESPECT TO ELECTRONIC RECORDS AND IDENTIFY THE TECHNOLOGY THE NOTARY PUBLIC INTENDS TO USE. IF THE SECRETARY OF STATE HAS ESTABLISHED STANDARDS FOR APPROVAL OF TECHNOLOGY PURSUANT TO SECTION 24-21-527, THE TECHNOLOGY MUST CONFORM TO THE STANDARDS. IF THE TECHNOLOGY CONFORMS TO THE STANDARDS, THE SECRETARY OF STATE SHALL APPROVE THE USE OF THE TECHNOLOGY.

(3) IN EVERY INSTANCE, THE ELECTRONIC SIGNATURE OF A NOTARY PUBLIC MUST CONTAIN OR BE ACCOMPANIED BY THE FOLLOWING ELEMENTS, ALL OF WHICH MUST BE IMMEDIATELY PERCEPTIBLE AND REPRODUCIBLE IN THE ELECTRONIC RECORD TO WHICH THE NOTARY'S ELECTRONIC SIGNATURE IS ATTACHED: THE NOTARY'S NAME, AS IT APPEARS ON THE NOTARY'S CERTIFICATE OF COMMISSION; THE NOTARY'S IDENTIFICATION NUMBER; THE WORDS "NOTARY PUBLIC" AND "STATE OF COLORADO"; A DOCUMENT AUTHENTICATION NUMBER ISSUED BY THE SECRETARY OF STATE; AND THE WORDS "MY COMMISSION EXPIRES" FOLLOWED BY THE EXPIRATION DATE OF THE NOTARY'S

COMMISSION. A NOTARY'S ELECTRONIC SIGNATURE MUST CONFORM TO ANY STANDARDS PROMULGATED BY THE SECRETARY OF STATE.

24-21-521. Commission as notary public - qualifications - no immunity or benefit. (1) AN INDIVIDUAL QUALIFIED UNDER SUBSECTION (3) OF THIS SECTION MAY APPLY TO THE SECRETARY OF STATE FOR A COMMISSION AS A NOTARY PUBLIC. THE APPLICANT SHALL COMPLY WITH AND PROVIDE THE INFORMATION REQUIRED BY RULES ESTABLISHED BY THE SECRETARY OF STATE AND PAY ANY APPLICATION FEE. IN ACCORDANCE WITH SECTION 24-21-111 (1), THE SECRETARY OF STATE MAY REQUIRE, AT THE SECRETARY OF STATE'S DISCRETION, THE APPLICATION REQUIRED BY THIS SECTION, AND ANY RENEWAL OF THE APPLICATION, TO BE MADE BY ELECTRONIC MEANS DESIGNATED BY THE SECRETARY OF STATE.

(2) IN ACCORDANCE WITH SECTION 42-1-211, THE DEPARTMENT OF STATE AND THE DEPARTMENT OF REVENUE SHALL ALLOW FOR THE EXCHANGE OF INFORMATION AND DATA COLLECTED BY THE SYSTEMS USED BY THE DEPARTMENTS TO COLLECT INFORMATION ON LEGAL NAMES AND SIGNATURES OF ALL APPLICANTS FOR DRIVER'S LICENSES OR STATE IDENTIFICATION CARDS.

(3) AN APPLICANT FOR A COMMISSION AS A NOTARY PUBLIC MUST:

(a) BE AT LEAST EIGHTEEN YEARS OF AGE;

(b) BE A CITIZEN OR PERMANENT LEGAL RESIDENT OF THE UNITED STATES OR OTHERWISE LAWFULLY PRESENT IN THE UNITED STATES;

(c) BE A RESIDENT OF OR HAVE A PLACE OF EMPLOYMENT OR PRACTICE IN THIS STATE;

(d) BE ABLE TO READ AND WRITE ENGLISH;

(e) NOT BE DISQUALIFIED TO RECEIVE A COMMISSION UNDER SECTION 24-21-523; AND

(f) HAVE PASSED THE EXAMINATION REQUIRED UNDER SECTION 24-21-522 (1).

(4) THE SECRETARY OF STATE SHALL VERIFY THE LAWFUL PRESENCE IN THE UNITED STATES OF EACH APPLICANT THROUGH THE VERIFICATION PROCESS OUTLINED IN SECTION 24-76.5-103 (4).

(5) BEFORE ISSUANCE OF A COMMISSION AS A NOTARY PUBLIC, AN APPLICANT FOR THE COMMISSION SHALL TAKE THE FOLLOWING AFFIRMATION IN THE PRESENCE OF A PERSON QUALIFIED TO ADMINISTER AN AFFIRMATION IN THIS STATE:

I, _____ (NAME OF APPLICANT), SOLEMNLY AFFIRM, UNDER THE PENALTY OF PERJURY IN THE SECOND DEGREE, AS DEFINED IN SECTION 18-8-503, COLORADO REVISED STATUTES, THAT I HAVE CAREFULLY READ THE NOTARY LAW OF THIS STATE, AND, IF APPOINTED AND COMMISSIONED AS A NOTARY PUBLIC, I WILL FAITHFULLY PERFORM, TO THE BEST OF MY ABILITY, ALL NOTARIAL ACTS IN CONFORMANCE WITH THE LAW.

_____
(SIGNATURE OF APPLICANT)
SUBSCRIBED AND AFFIRMED BEFORE ME THIS _____ DAY OF _____, 20___

_____
(OFFICIAL SIGNATURE AND SEAL OF PERSON QUALIFIED TO ADMINISTER AFFIRMATION)

(6) ON COMPLIANCE WITH THIS SECTION, THE SECRETARY OF STATE SHALL ISSUE A COMMISSION AS A NOTARY PUBLIC TO AN APPLICANT FOR A TERM OF FOUR YEARS, UNLESS REVOKED IN ACCORDANCE WITH SECTION 24-21-523. AN APPLICANT WHO HAS BEEN DENIED APPOINTMENT AND COMMISSION MAY APPEAL THE DECISION IN ACCORDANCE WITH ARTICLE 4 OF THIS TITLE 24.

(7) A COMMISSION TO ACT AS A NOTARY PUBLIC AUTHORIZES THE NOTARY PUBLIC TO PERFORM NOTARIAL ACTS. THE COMMISSION DOES NOT PROVIDE THE NOTARY PUBLIC ANY IMMUNITY OR BENEFIT CONFERRED BY LAW OF THIS STATE ON PUBLIC OFFICIALS OR. EMPLOYEES.

24-21-522. Examination of notary public. (1) AN APPLICANT FOR A COMMISSION AS A NOTARY PUBLIC WHO DOES NOT HOLD A COMMISSION IN THIS STATE MUST PASS AN EXAMINATION ADMINISTERED BY THE SECRETARY OF STATE OR AN ENTITY APPROVED BY THE SECRETARY OF STATE. THE EXAMINATION MUST BE BASED ON THE COURSE OF STUDY DESCRIBED IN SUBSECTION (2) OF THIS SECTION.

(2) THE SECRETARY OF STATE OR AN ENTITY APPROVED BY THE SECRETARY OF STATE SHALL OFFER REGULARLY A COURSE OF STUDY TO APPLICANTS WHO DO NOT HOLD COMMISSIONS AS NOTARIES PUBLIC IN THIS STATE. THE COURSE MUST COVER THE LAWS, RULES, PROCEDURES, AND ETHICS RELEVANT TO NOTARIAL ACTS. THE OFFICE OF THE SECRETARY OF STATE MAY ENTER INTO A CONTRACT WITH A PRIVATE CONTRACTOR OR CONTRACTORS TO CONDUCT NOTARY TRAINING PROGRAMS. THE CONTRACTOR OR CONTRACTORS MAY CHARGE A FEE FOR ANY SUCH TRAINING PROGRAM.

24-21-523. Grounds to deny, refuse to renew, revoke, suspend, or condition commission of notary public. (1) THE SECRETARY OF STATE MAY DENY, REFUSE TO RENEW, REVOKE, SUSPEND, OR IMPOSE A CONDITION ON A COMMISSION AS NOTARY PUBLIC FOR:

(a) FAILURE TO COMPLY WITH THIS PART 5;

(b) A SUBSTANTIAL AND MATERIAL MISSTATEMENT OR OMISSION OF FACT IN THE APPLICATION FOR A COMMISSION AS A NOTARY PUBLIC SUBMITTED TO THE SECRETARY OF STATE;

(c) NOTWITHSTANDING SECTION 24-5-101, A CONVICTION OF THE APPLICANT OR NOTARY PUBLIC OF ANY FELONY OR, IN THE PRIOR FIVE YEARS, A MISDEMEANOR INVOLVING DISHONESTY;

(d) A FINDING AGAINST, OR ADMISSION OF LIABILITY BY, THE APPLICANT OR NOTARY PUBLIC IN ANY LEGAL PROCEEDING OR DISCIPLINARY ACTION BASED ON THE APPLICANT'S OR NOTARY PUBLIC'S FRAUD, DISHONESTY, OR DECEIT;

(e) FAILURE BY THE NOTARY PUBLIC TO DISCHARGE ANY DUTY REQUIRED OF A NOTARY PUBLIC, WHETHER BY THIS PART 5, RULES OF THE SECRETARY OF STATE, OR ANY FEDERAL OR STATE LAW;

(f) USE OF FALSE OR MISLEADING ADVERTISING OR REPRESENTATION BY THE NOTARY PUBLIC REPRESENTING THAT THE NOTARY HAS A DUTY, RIGHT, OR PRIVILEGE THAT THE NOTARY DOES NOT HAVE;

(g) VIOLATION BY THE NOTARY PUBLIC OF A RULE OF THE SECRETARY OF STATE REGARDING A NOTARY PUBLIC;

(h) DENIAL, REFUSAL TO RENEW, REVOCATION, SUSPENSION, OR CONDITIONING OF A NOTARY PUBLIC COMMISSION IN ANOTHER STATE;

(i) A FINDING BY A COURT OF THIS STATE THAT THE APPLICANT OR NOTARY PUBLIC HAS ENGAGED IN THE UNAUTHORIZED PRACTICE OF LAW;

(j) FAILURE TO COMPLY WITH ANY TERM OF SUSPENSION OR CONDITION IMPOSED ON THE COMMISSION OF A NOTARY PUBLIC UNDER THIS SECTION; OR

(k) PERFORMANCE OF ANY NOTARIAL ACT WHILE NOT CURRENTLY COMMISSIONED BY THE SECRETARY OF STATE.

(2) WHENEVER THE SECRETARY OF STATE OR THE SECRETARY OF STATE'S DESIGNEE BELIEVES THAT A VIOLATION OF THIS PART 5 HAS OCCURRED, THE SECRETARY OF STATE OR THE SECRETARY OF STATE'S DESIGNEE MAY INVESTIGATE THE VIOLATION. THE SECRETARY OF STATE OR THE SECRETARY OF STATE'S DESIGNEE MAY ALSO INVESTIGATE POSSIBLE VIOLATIONS OF THIS PART 5 UPON A SIGNED COMPLAINT FROM ANY PERSON.

(3) IF THE SECRETARY OF STATE DENIES, REFUSES TO RENEW, REVOKES, SUSPENDS, OR IMPOSES CONDITIONS ON A COMMISSION AS A NOTARY PUBLIC, THE APPLICANT OR NOTARY PUBLIC IS ENTITLED TO TIMELY NOTICE AND HEARING IN ACCORDANCE WITH THE "STATE ADMINISTRATIVE PROCEDURE ACT", ARTICLE 4 OF THIS TITLE 24.

(4) WHEN A COMPLAINT OR INVESTIGATION RESULTS IN A FINDING OF MISCONDUCT THAT, IN THE SECRETARY OF STATE'S DISCRETION, DOES NOT WARRANT INITIATION OF A DISCIPLINARY PROCEEDING, THE SECRETARY OF STATE MAY TAKE NONDISCIPLINARY ACTION. FOR THE PURPOSES OF THIS SUBSECTION (4), NONDISCIPLINARY ACTION INCLUDES THE ISSUANCE OF A LETTER OF ADMONITION, WHICH MAY BE PLACED IN THE NOTARY PUBLIC'S FILE.

(5) THE AUTHORITY OF THE SECRETARY OF STATE TO DENY, REFUSE TO RENEW, SUSPEND, REVOKE, OR IMPOSE CONDITIONS ON A COMMISSION AS A NOTARY PUBLIC DOES NOT PREVENT A PERSON FROM SEEKING AND OBTAINING OTHER CRIMINAL OR CIVIL REMEDIES PROVIDED BY LAW.

(6) A PERSON WHOSE NOTARY COMMISSION HAS BEEN REVOKED PURSUANT TO THIS PART 5 MAY NOT APPLY FOR OR RECEIVE A COMMISSION AND APPOINTMENT AS A NOTARY.

24-21-524. Database of notaries public. (1) THE SECRETARY OF STATE SHALL MAINTAIN AN ELECTRONIC DATABASE OF NOTARIES PUBLIC:

(a) THROUGH WHICH A PERSON MAY VERIFY THE AUTHORITY OF A NOTARY PUBLIC TO PERFORM NOTARIAL ACTS; AND

(b) WHICH INDICATES WHETHER A NOTARY PUBLIC HAS NOTIFIED THE SECRETARY OF STATE THAT THE NOTARY PUBLIC WILL BE PERFORMING NOTARIAL ACTS ON ELECTRONIC RECORDS.

24-21-525. Prohibited acts. (1) A COMMISSION AS A NOTARY PUBLIC DOES NOT AUTHORIZE AN INDIVIDUAL TO:

(a) ASSIST PERSONS IN DRAFTING LEGAL RECORDS, GIVE LEGAL ADVICE, OR OTHERWISE PRACTICE LAW;

(b) ACT AS AN IMMIGRATION CONSULTANT OR AN EXPERT ON IMMIGRATION MATTERS;

(c) REPRESENT A PERSON IN A JUDICIAL OR ADMINISTRATIVE PROCEEDING RELATING TO IMMIGRATION TO THE UNITED STATES, UNITED STATES CITIZENSHIP, OR RELATED MATTERS; OR

(d) RECEIVE COMPENSATION FOR PERFORMING ANY OF THE ACTIVITIES LISTED IN THIS SUBSECTION (1).

(2) A NOTARY PUBLIC SHALL NOT ENGAGE IN FALSE OR DECEPTIVE ADVERTISING.

(3) A NOTARY PUBLIC, OTHER THAN AN ATTORNEY LICENSED TO PRACTICE LAW IN THIS STATE, SHALL NOT USE THE TERM "NOTARIO" OR "NOTARIO PUBLICO".

(4) A NOTARY PUBLIC, OTHER THAN AN ATTORNEY LICENSED TO PRACTICE LAW IN THIS STATE, SHALL NOT ADVERTISE OR REPRESENT THAT THE NOTARY PUBLIC MAY ASSIST PERSONS IN DRAFTING LEGAL RECORDS, GIVE LEGAL ADVICE, OR OTHERWISE PRACTICE LAW. IF A NOTARY PUBLIC WHO IS NOT AN ATTORNEY LICENSED TO PRACTICE LAW IN THIS STATE IN ANY MANNER ADVERTISES OR REPRESENTS THAT THE NOTARY PUBLIC OFFERS NOTARIAL SERVICES, WHETHER ORALLY OR IN A RECORD, INCLUDING BROADCAST MEDIA, PRINT MEDIA, AND THE INTERNET, THE NOTARY PUBLIC SHALL INCLUDE THE FOLLOWING STATEMENT, OR AN ALTERNATE STATEMENT AUTHORIZED OR REQUIRED BY THE SECRETARY OF STATE, IN THE ADVERTISEMENT OR REPRESENTATION, PROMINENTLY AND IN EACH LANGUAGE USED IN THE ADVERTISEMENT OR REPRESENTATION: "I AM NOT AN ATTORNEY LICENSED TO PRACTICE LAW IN THE STATE OF COLORADO AND I MAY NOT GIVE LEGAL ADVICE OR ACCEPT FEES FOR LEGAL ADVICE. I AM NOT AN IMMIGRATION CONSULTANT, NOR AM I AN EXPERT ON IMMIGRATION MATTERS. IF YOU SUSPECT FRAUD, YOU MAY CONTACT THE COLORADO ATTORNEY GENERAL'S OFFICE OR THE COLORADO SUPREME COURT." IF THE FORM OF ADVERTISEMENT OR REPRESENTATION IS NOT BROADCAST MEDIA, PRINT MEDIA, OR THE INTERNET AND DOES NOT PERMIT INCLUSION OF THE STATEMENT REQUIRED BY THIS SUBSECTION (4) BECAUSE OF SIZE, IT MUST BE DISPLAYED PROMINENTLY OR PROVIDED AT THE PLACE OF PERFORMANCE OF THE NOTARIAL ACT BEFORE THE NOTARIAL ACT IS PERFORMED.

(5) A NOTARY PUBLIC, OTHER THAN AN ATTORNEY LICENSED TO PRACTICE LAW IN THIS STATE, SHALL NOT ENGAGE IN CONDUCT THAT CONSTITUTES A DECEPTIVE TRADE PRACTICE PURSUANT TO SECTION 6-1-727.

(6) EXCEPT AS OTHERWISE ALLOWED BY LAW, A NOTARY PUBLIC SHALL NOT WITHHOLD ACCESS TO OR POSSESSION OF AN ORIGINAL RECORD PROVIDED BY A PERSON THAT SEEKS PERFORMANCE OF A NOTARIAL ACT BY THE NOTARY PUBLIC.

(7) A NOTARY PUBLIC SHALL NOT PERFORM ANY NOTARIAL ACT WITH RESPECT TO A RECORD THAT IS BLANK OR THAT CONTAINS UNFILLED BLANKS IN ITS TEXT.

24-21-526. Validity of notarial acts. EXCEPT AS OTHERWISE PROVIDED IN SECTION 24-21-504 (2), THE FAILURE OF A NOTARIAL OFFICER TO PERFORM A DUTY OR MEET A REQUIREMENT SPECIFIED IN THIS PART 5 DOES NOT INVALIDATE A NOTARIAL ACT PERFORMED BY THE NOTARIAL OFFICER. THE VALIDITY OF A NOTARIAL ACT UNDER THIS PART 5 DOES NOT PREVENT AN AGGRIEVED PERSON FROM SEEKING TO INVALIDATE THE RECORD OR TRANSACTION THAT IS THE SUBJECT OF THE NOTARIAL ACT OR FROM SEEKING OTHER REMEDIES BASED ON LAW OF THIS STATE OTHER THAN THIS PART 5 OR LAW OF THE

UNITED STATES. THIS SECTION DOES NOT VALIDATE A PURPORTED NOTARIAL ACT PERFORMED BY AN INDIVIDUAL WHO DOES NOT HAVE THE AUTHORITY TO PERFORM NOTARIAL ACTS.

24-21-527. Rules. (1) THE SECRETARY OF STATE MAY ADOPT RULES TO IMPLEMENT THIS PART 5 IN ACCORDANCE WITH ARTICLE 4 OF THIS TITLE 24. RULES ADOPTED REGARDING THE PERFORMANCE OF NOTARIAL ACTS WITH RESPECT TO ELECTRONIC RECORDS MAY NOT REQUIRE, OR ACCORD GREATER LEGAL STATUS OR EFFECT TO, THE IMPLEMENTATION OR APPLICATION OF A SPECIFIC TECHNOLOGY OR TECHNICAL SPECIFICATION. THE RULES MAY:

(a) PRESCRIBE THE MANNER OF PERFORMING NOTARIAL ACTS REGARDING TANGIBLE AND ELECTRONIC RECORDS;

(b) INCLUDE PROVISIONS TO ENSURE THAT ANY CHANGE TO OR TAMPERING WITH A RECORD BEARING A CERTIFICATE OF A NOTARIAL ACT IS SELF-EVIDENT;

(c) INCLUDE PROVISIONS TO ENSURE INTEGRITY IN THE CREATION, TRANSMITTAL, STORAGE, OR AUTHENTICATION OF ELECTRONIC RECORDS OR SIGNATURES;

(d) PRESCRIBE THE PROCESS OF GRANTING, RENEWING, CONDITIONING, DENYING, SUSPENDING, OR REVOKING A NOTARY PUBLIC COMMISSION AND ASSURING THE TRUSTWORTHINESS OF AN INDIVIDUAL HOLDING A COMMISSION AS NOTARY PUBLIC, INCLUDING RULES FOR USE OF THE ELECTRONIC FILING SYSTEM;

(e) INCLUDE PROVISIONS TO PREVENT FRAUD OR MISTAKE IN THE PERFORMANCE OF NOTARIAL ACTS; AND

(f) PROVIDE FOR THE ADMINISTRATION OF THE EXAMINATION UNDER SECTION 24-21-522 (1) AND THE COURSE OF STUDY UNDER SECTION 24-21-522 (2).

(2) IN ADOPTING, AMENDING, OR REPEALING RULES ABOUT NOTARIAL ACTS WITH RESPECT TO ELECTRONIC RECORDS, THE SECRETARY OF STATE SHALL CONSIDER, SO FAR AS IS CONSISTENT WITH THIS PART 5:

(a) THE MOST RECENT STANDARDS REGARDING ELECTRONIC RECORDS PROMULGATED BY NATIONAL BODIES, SUCH AS THE NATIONAL ASSOCIATION OF SECRETARIES OF STATE;

(b) STANDARDS, PRACTICES, AND CUSTOMS OF OTHER JURISDICTIONS THAT SUBSTANTIALLY ENACT THIS PART 5; AND

(c) THE VIEWS OF GOVERNMENTAL OFFICIALS AND ENTITIES AND OTHER INTERESTED PERSONS.

24-21-528. Disposition of fees. (1) THE SECRETARY OF STATE SHALL COLLECT ALL FEES PURSUANT TO THIS ARTICLE 21 IN THE MANNER REQUIRED BY SECTION 24-21-104 (3) AND SHALL TRANSMIT THEM TO THE STATE TREASURER, WHO SHALL CREDIT THEM TO THE DEPARTMENT OF STATE CASH FUND CREATED IN SECTION 24-21-104 (3)(b).

(2) THE GENERAL ASSEMBLY SHALL MAKE ANNUAL APPROPRIATIONS FROM THE DEPARTMENT OF STATE CASH FUND FOR EXPENDITURES OF THE SECRETARY OF STATE INCURRED IN THE PERFORMANCE OF THE SECRETARY OF STATE'S DUTIES UNDER THIS PART 5.

24-21-529. Notary's fees. (1) EXCEPT AS SPECIFIED IN SUBSECTION (2) OF THIS SECTION, THE FEES OF A NOTARY PUBLIC MAY BE, BUT MUST NOT EXCEED, FIVE DOLLARS FOR EACH DOCUMENT ATTESTED BY A PERSON BEFORE A NOTARY, EXCEPT AS OTHERWISE PROVIDED BY LAW. THE FEE FOR EACH SUCH DOCUMENT MUST INCLUDE ALL DUTIES AND FUNCTIONS REQUIRED TO COMPLETE THE NOTARIAL ACT IN ACCORDANCE WITH THIS PART 5.

(2) IN LIEU OF THE FEE AUTHORIZED IN SUBSECTION (1) OF THIS SECTION, A NOTARY PUBLIC MAY CHARGE A FEE, NOT TO EXCEED TEN DOLLARS, FOR THE NOTARY'S ELECTRONIC SIGNATURE.

24-21-530. Change of name or address. A NOTARY PUBLIC SHALL NOTIFY THE SECRETARY OF STATE WITHIN THIRTY DAYS AFTER HE OR SHE CHANGES HIS OR HER NAME, BUSINESS ADDRESS, OR RESIDENTIAL ADDRESS. IN THE CASE OF A NAME CHANGE, THE NOTARY PUBLIC SHALL INCLUDE A SAMPLE OF THE NOTARY'S HANDWRITTEN OFFICIAL SIGNATURE ON THE NOTICE. PURSUANT TO SECTION 24-21-104 (3), THE SECRETARY OF STATE SHALL DETERMINE THE AMOUNT OF, AND COLLECT, THE FEE, PAYABLE TO THE SECRETARY OF STATE, FOR RECORDING NOTICE OF CHANGE OF NAME OR ADDRESS.

24-21-531. Official misconduct by a notary public - liability of notary or surety. (1) A NOTARY PUBLIC WHO KNOWINGLY AND WILLFULLY VIOLATES THE DUTIES IMPOSED BY THIS PART 5 COMMITS OFFICIAL MISCONDUCT AND IS GUILTY OF A CLASS 2 MISDEMEANOR.

(2) A NOTARY PUBLIC AND THE SURETY OR SURETIES ON HIS OR HER BOND ARE LIABLE TO THE PERSONS INVOLVED FOR ALL DAMAGES PROXIMATELY CAUSED BY THE NOTARY'S OFFICIAL MISCONDUCT.

(3) NOTHING IN THIS PART 5 SHALL BE CONSTRUED TO DENY A NOTARY PUBLIC THE RIGHT TO OBTAIN A SURETY BOND OR INSURANCE ON A VOLUNTARY BASIS TO PROVIDE COVERAGE FOR LIABILITY.

24-21-532. Willful impersonation. A PERSON WHO ACTS AS, OR OTHERWISE WILLFULLY IMPERSONATES, A NOTARY PUBLIC WHILE NOT LAWFULLY APPOINTED AND COMMISSIONED TO PERFORM NOTARIAL ACTS IS GUILTY OF A CLASS 2 MISDEMEANOR AND SHALL BE PUNISHED AS SPECIFIED IN SECTION 18-1.3-501.

24-21-533. Wrongful possession of journal or seal. A PERSON WHO UNLAWFULLY POSSESSES AND USES A NOTARY'S JOURNAL, AN OFFICIAL SEAL, A NOTARY'S ELECTRONIC SIGNATURE, OR ANY PAPERS, COPIES, OR ELECTRONIC RECORDS RELATING TO NOTARIAL ACTS IS GUILTY OF A CLASS 3 MISDEMEANOR AND SHALL BE PUNISHED AS SPECIFIED IN SECTION 18-1.3-501.

24-21-534. Certification restrictions. (1) THE SECRETARY OF STATE MAY ISSUE CERTIFICATES OR APOSTILLES ATTESTING TO THE AUTHENTICITY OF A NOTARIAL ACT PERFORMED BY A COMMISSIONED NOTARY PUBLIC.

(2) THE SECRETARY OF STATE SHALL NOT CERTIFY A SIGNATURE OF A NOTARY PUBLIC ON:

(a) A RECORD THAT IS NOT PROPERLY NOTARIZED IN ACCORDANCE WITH THE REQUIREMENTS OF THIS PART 5;

(b) A RECORD:

(I) REGARDING ALLEGIANCE TO A GOVERNMENT OR JURISDICTION;

(II) RELATING TO THE RELINQUISHMENT OR RENUNCIATION OF CITIZENSHIP, SOVEREIGNTY, IN ITINERE STATUS OR WORLD SERVICE AUTHORITY; OR

(III) SETTING FORTH OR IMPLYING FOR THE BEARER A CLAIM OF IMMUNITY FROM THE LAW OF THIS STATE OR FEDERAL LAW.

24-21-535. Notary public commission in effect. A COMMISSION AS A NOTARY PUBLIC IN EFFECT ON THE EFFECTIVE DATE OF THIS PART 5 CONTINUES UNTIL ITS DATE OF EXPIRATION. A NOTARY PUBLIC WHO APPLIES TO RENEW A COMMISSION AS A NOTARY PUBLIC ON OR AFTER THE EFFECTIVE DATE OF THIS PART 5 IS SUBJECT TO AND SHALL COMPLY WITH THIS PART 5. A NOTARY PUBLIC, IN PERFORMING NOTARIAL ACTS AFTER THE EFFECTIVE DATE OF THIS PART 5, SHALL COMPLY WITH THIS PART 5.

24-21-536. Savings clause. THIS PART 5 DOES NOT AFFECT THE VALIDITY OR EFFECT OF A NOTARIAL ACT PERFORMED BEFORE THE EFFECTIVE DATE OF THIS PART 5.

24-21-537. Uniformity of application and construction. IN APPLYING AND CONSTRUING THIS PART 5, CONSIDERATION MUST BE GIVEN TO THE NEED TO PROMOTE UNIFORMITY OF THE LAW WITH RESPECT TO ITS SUBJECT MATTER AMONG STATES THAT ENACT IT.

24-21-538. Relation to "Electronic Signatures in Global and National Commerce Act". THIS PART 5 MODIFIES, LIMITS, AND SUPERSEDES THE "ELECTRONIC SIGNATURES IN GLOBAL AND NATIONAL COMMERCE ACT", 15 U.S.C. SEC. 7001 ET SEQ., BUT DOES NOT MODIFY, LIMIT, OR SUPERSEDE SECTION 101 (c) OF THAT ACT, 15 U.S.C. SEC. 7001 (c), OR AUTHORIZE ELECTRONIC DELIVERY OF ANY OF THE NOTICES DESCRIBED IN SECTION 103 (b) OF THAT ACT, 15 U.S.C. SEC. 7003 (b).

24-21-539. Effective date. THIS PART 5 TAKES EFFECT ON JULY 1, 2018.

24-21-540. Repeal. THIS PART 5 IS REPEALED, EFFECTIVE SEPTEMBER 1, 2023. BEFORE ITS REPEAL, THIS PART 5 IS SCHEDULED FOR REVIEW IN ACCORDANCE WITH SECTION 24-34-104.

SECTION 3. In Colorado Revised Statutes, 24-34-104, amend (14)(a) introductory portion and (24)(a) introductory portion; repeal (14)(a)(VII); and add (24)(a)(IV) as follows:

24-34-104. General assembly review of regulatory agencies and functions for repeal, continuation, or reestablishment - legislative declaration - repeal. (14) (a) The following agencies, functions, or both, ARE SCHEDULED FOR repeal on July 1, 2018:

(24) (a) The following agencies, functions, or both, roams ARE SCHEDULED FOR repeal on September 1, 2023:

(IV) THE APPOINTMENT OF NOTARIES PUBLIC THROUGH THE SECRETARY OF STATE IN ACCORDANCE WITH PART 5 OF ARTICLE 21 OF THIS TITLE 24;

SECTION 4. In Colorado Revised Statutes, 6-1-105, amend (1)(vv) as follows:

6-1-105. Deceptive trade practices. (1) A person engages in a deceptive trade practice when, in the course of the person's business, vocation, or occupation, the person:

(vv) Violates section 24-21-523 (1)(f) OR (1)(i) OR 24-21-525 (3), (4), OR (5);

SECTION 5. In Colorado Revised Statutes, 6-1-727, amend (3)(e)(III)(A) as follows:

6-1-727. Immigration-related services provided by nonattorneys - deceptive trade practice. (3) Prohibited practices - assistance with immigration matters - permitted practices. (e) Notwithstanding paragraphs (a) to (d) of this subsection (3), a person other than a person listed in subparagraph (I) or (II) of paragraph (a) of this subsection (3) may:

(III) Offer other immigration-related services that:

(A) Are not prohibited under this subsection (3), section 24-21-523 (1)(f) OR (1)(i) OR 24-21-525 (3), (4), OR (5), or any other provision of law;

8 CCR 1505-11
Notary Program Rules
Adopted May 10, 2018

Current 8 CCR 1505-11 is amended as follows: Amendments to Rule 1 concerning definitions:

1.4 "DAN" means the unique document authentication number issued by the Secretary of State and required by SECTION 24-21-520(3), C.R.S., for electronic notarizations.

New Rules 1.7 and 1.8

1.7 "LEGAL PROCEEDING OR DISCIPLINARY ACTION BASED ON THE APPLICANT'S OR NOTARY PUBLIC'S FRAUD, DISHONESTY, OR DECEIT" IN SECTION 24-21-523(1)(D), C.R.S., MEANS ANY CIVIL OR CRIMINAL MATTER CONDUCTED EITHER JUDICIALLY OR ADMINISTRATIVELY CONCERNING ACTIVITIES INVOLVING FRAUD, DECEIT, OR THE OTHER VIOLATIONS LISTED IN RULE 1.8.

1.8 "MISDEMEANOR INVOLVING DISHONESTY" IN SECTION 24-21-523(1)(C), C.R.S., MEANS A VIOLATION OF, OR A CONSPIRACY TO VIOLATE, A CIVIL OR CRIMINAL LAW INVOLVING FRAUD, DISHONESTY, BRIBERY, PERJURY, LARCENY, THEFT, ROBBERY, EXTORTION, FORGERY, COUNTERFEITING, EMBEZZLEMENT, MISAPPROPRIATION OF PROPERTY, OR ANY OTHER OFFENSE ADVERSELY AFFECTING A PERSON'S FITNESS TO SERVE AS A NOTARY PUBLIC.

1.9 "New applicant" means a person seeking a commission as a Colorado notary for the first time or a formerly commissioned notary in Colorado whose commission has been expired for more than 30 days.

Amendments to Rule 2 concerning notary commissions:

[Regarding filing and training requirements: New Rule 2.1.3. Current Rules 2.1.3, 2.1.4, and 2.1.5 are renumbered as Rules 2.1.4, 2.1.5, and 2.1.6. New Rule 2.1.6(a) is amended.]

2.1.3 NO MORE THAN 90 DAYS BEFORE RENEWING A COMMISSION, A NOTARY

MUST SUCCESSFULLY COMPLETE THE RENEWAL TRAINING AND PASS THE EXAM ADMINISTERED BY THE SECRETARY OF STATE.

2.1.4 The Secretary of State will grant credit only for completion of courses offered by an approved vendor, an approved course provider, or the Secretary of State.

2.1.5 The Secretary of State may require a notary who has committed misconduct meriting a disciplinary proceeding to retake and successfully complete the training and exam.

2.1.6 Examination. The Secretary of State's open book examination will test the applicant's understanding of notary duties contained in the following:

(a) Title 24, Article 21, PART 5 (REVISED UNIFORM LAW ON NOTARIAL ACTS) of the Colorado Revised Statutes;

(b) Title 38, Article 30 (Titles and Interests) of the Colorado Revised Statutes;

(c) Title 1, Article 40 (Initiative and Referendum) of the Colorado Revised Statutes; and

(d) The Official Notary Handbook published by the Secretary of State.

[Amendments to current Rule 2.2.1, concerning electronic notarization]

2.2.1 A notary must submit a notice of intent on the approved form and receive approval from the Secretary of State before the notary may electronically notarize a document. A new applicant may file the intent at the time of application but may only electronically notarize a document after he or she has been commissioned and approved. A NOTARY MAY CHOOSE TO EITHER USE A DAN AS THE NOTARY'S ELECTRONIC SIGNATURE OR ADOPT A DIFFERENT ELECTRONIC SIGNATURE WHICH THE NOTARY MUST ALWAYS USE IN CONJUNCTION WITH A DAN. If the applicant intends to use a different electronic signature than a DAN, the applicant must attach an example of the electronic signature, a description of the electronic signature technology, and contact information for the technology's supplier or vendor. A notary must notify the Secretary of State of all electronic signature changes.

[Current Rules 2.2.2 and 2.2.3 are repealed. Current Rules 2.2.4 and 2.2.5 are renumbered as Rules 2.2.2 and 2.2.3]

2.2.2 A notary must:

(a) Use a different DAN for each electronic notarization;

(b) Take reasonable measures to secure assigned DANs against another person's access or use and must not permit such access or use; and

(c) Request new DANs to replace lost or stolen DANs after notifying the Secretary in the same manner as for a journal or seal.

2.2.3 A notary must verify that the document signer has adopted an electronic signature to function as his or her signature before electronically notarizing a document.

[Current Rule 2.2.6 is renumbered as Rule 2.2.4 and amended.]

2.2.4 Expiration of the Secretary of State's approval to notarize electronically

(a) Approval automatically expires:

(1) Upon revocation, expiration, or resignation of the notary's commission;

(2) 30 days after the notary's name changes unless the notary previously submitted a name change.

(3) Upon conviction of a felony;

(4) UPON CONVICTION OF A MISDEMEANOR INVOLVING DISHONESTY;

(5) If the notary NO LONGER HAS A PLACE OF EMPLOYMENT OR PRACTICE OR A RESIDENTIAL ADDRESS IN THE STATE OF COLORADO; or

(6) Upon the expiration or revocation of the technology described in the notification.

(b) If approval expires, the notary or the notary's authorized representative must destroy all electronic notarization software and unused DANs unless:

(1) The notary's commission expired; and

(2) Within 30 days of the commission's expiration, the Secretary of State recommissions the notary and the notary reregisters his or her electronic signature.

Amendments to Rule 3, concerning notary trainer requirements:

[Amendments to current Rule 3.1.1(b), concerning course provider applicant requirements:]

3.1.1 A course provider applicant must:

[No amendments to current Rule 3.1.1(a)]

(b) Attend IN-PERSON OR ONLINE training provided by the Secretary of State.

[Amendments to current Rule 3.2.1(a), concerning vendor-specific requirements:]

3.2.1 The Secretary of State must approve a vendor's proposed curriculum before a vendor may offer a notary training course. Curriculum must be based on:

(a) The Colorado REVISED UNIFORM LAW ON NOTARIAL ACTS including but not limited to: the physical presence requirement, duty not to notarize a blank document, duty to use a notarial certificate, disqualifying interest, application procedures, resignation requirements, duty to maintain a journal of notarial acts, revocation proceedings, liability, identification of signers, role of the notary, and official misconduct; and

[No amendments to current Rule 3.2.1(b)]

[Current Rule 3.2.2(c), concerning seal of accreditation, is amended.]

(c) A seal of accreditation expires four years after issuance. To renew accreditation, a vendor must submit FOR REAPPROVAL A DETAILED CURRICULUM; COPIES OF ANY COURSE HANDOUT MATERIALS, WORKBOOKS, AND TESTS; AND the required form and fee.

[Current Rule 3.5 is amended.]

3.5 Duty to revise training. Approved vendors and course providers must revise approved courses of instruction as necessary to ensure that the courses accurately reflect current Colorado law. APPROVED VENDORS AND COURSE PROVIDERS MUST SUBMIT NOTICE OF REVISED TRAINING AND COPIES OF THE REVISIONS TO THE SECRETARY OF STATE FOR REVIEW AND APPROVAL IN A FORMAT THAT SATISFIES RULE 3.4, BEFORE OFFERING THE REVISED TRAINING TO THE PUBLIC.

[New Rule 4.]

RULE 4. NOTARY JOURNAL REQUIREMENTS

4.1 IF A CURRENT OR FORMER NOTARY LEAVES THE NOTARY JOURNAL WITH THE NOTARY'S FIRM OR EMPLOYER, AS AUTHORIZED BY SECTION 24-21-519(10)(A), C.R.S., THE NOTARY MUST NOTIFY THE SECRETARY OF STATE BY ELECTRONICALLY SUBMITTING THE REQUIRED FORM WITHIN 30 DAYS. THE NOTARY MUST PROVIDE THE NOTARY'S FIRM OR EMPLOYER WITH A COPY OF THE REQUIRED FORM AT THE TIME OF ELECTRONIC SUBMISSION TO THE SECRETARY OF STATE.

4.2 A FIRM OR EMPLOYER IN POSSESSION OF A NOTARY'S JOURNAL HAS THE SAME RESPONSIBILITY AS A NOTARY TO:

4.2.1 KEEP THE JOURNAL SECURE AS DETAILED IN SECTION 24-21-519(4), C.R.S.;

4.2.2 PROVIDE A COPY OF A REQUESTED TRANSACTION TO A MEMBER OF THE PUBLIC PER SECTION 24-21-519(5), C.R.S, BUT WITHOUT CERTIFYING THE COPY OR CHARGING A NOTARY FEE;

4.2.3 PROVIDE THE JOURNAL TO THE SECRETARY OF STATE FOR AUDITING OR INSPECTION WITHOUT RESTRICTION PER SECTION 24-21-519(6), C.R.S.;

4.2.4 PROVIDE THE JOURNAL TO A CERTIFIED PEACE OFFICER PER SECTION 24-21-519(7), C.R.S.; AND **4.2.5** NOTIFY THE SECRETARY OF STATE IF THE JOURNAL IS LOST OR STOLEN PER SECTION 24-21-519(8), C.R.S.

4.3 A FIRM OR EMPLOYER IN POSSESSION OF A NOTARY'S JOURNAL MAY:

4.3.1 RETAIN THE JOURNAL INDEFINITELY; OR

4.3.2 TRANSMIT THE JOURNAL TO THE COLORADO STATE ARCHIVES AND NOTIFY THE SECRETARY OF STATE PER SECTION 24-21-519(10)(A)(I) AND (B), C.R.S.

COLORADO REVISED STATUTES
TITLE 15
PROBATE, TRUSTS, AND FIDUCIARIES
ARTICLE 1
FIDUCIARY

15-1-1302. Statutory form of power of attorney.

(1) Form.

(a) The form set forth in paragraph (b) of this subsection (1) may be known as the "statutory power of attorney for property" and may be used to grant an agent powers with respect to property and financial and other matters of the principal. When a power of attorney in substantially the form set forth in paragraph (b) of this subsection (1) is used, including the notice paragraphs in capital letters at the beginning of the form and the notarized form of acknowledgment at the end of the form, it shall have the meaning and effect prescribed in this part 13. The issue of whether a power of attorney meets the requirements of a statutory power of attorney for property shall not be affected if one or more of the categories of optional powers listed in the form are withheld or if the form includes specific limitations on or additions to the agent's powers, as permitted by the form. Nothing in this part 13 shall invalidate or bar any principal's use of any other or different form of power of attorney for property. Any nonstatutory power of attorney for property must be executed by the principal and must designate the agent and the agent's powers, but need not be acknowledged or conform in any other respect to the statutory power of attorney for property.

(b) The following statutory power of attorney for property form is legally sufficient:

COLORADO STATUTORY POWER OF ATTORNEY FOR PROPERTY

NOTICE: UNLESS YOU LIMIT THE POWER IN THIS DOCUMENT, THIS DOCUMENT GIVES YOUR AGENT THE POWER TO ACT FOR YOU, WITHOUT YOUR CONSENT, IN ANY WAY THAT YOU COULD ACT FOR YOURSELF. THE POWERS GRANTED BY THIS DOCUMENT ARE BROAD AND SWEEPING. THEY ARE EXPLAINED IN THE "UNIFORM STATUTORY FORM POWER OF ATTORNEY ACT", PART 13 OF ARTICLE 1 OF TITLE 15, COLORADO REVISED STATUTES, AND PART 6 OF ARTICLE 14 OF TITLE 15, COLORADO REVISED STATUTES. IF YOU HAVE ANY QUESTIONS ABOUT THESE POWERS, OBTAIN COMPETENT LEGAL ADVICE. THIS DOCUMENT DOES NOT AUTHORIZE ANYONE TO MAKE MEDICAL OR OTHER HEALTHCARE DECISIONS FOR YOU. YOU MAY REVOKE THIS POWER OF ATTORNEY IF YOU LATER WISH TO DO SO.

THE PURPOSE OF THIS POWER OF ATTORNEY IS TO GIVE THE PERSON YOU DESIGNATE (YOUR "AGENT") BROAD POWERS TO HANDLE YOUR PROPERTY AND AFFAIRS, WHICH MAY INCLUDE POWERS TO PLEDGE, SELL, OR OTHERWISE DISPOSE OF ANY REAL OR PERSONAL PROPERTY WITHOUT ADVANCE NOTICE TO YOU OR APPROVAL BY YOU. THIS FORM DOES NOT IMPOSE A DUTY ON YOUR AGENT TO EXERCISE GRANTED POWERS; BUT WHEN POWERS ARE EXERCISED, YOUR AGENT MUST USE DUE CARE TO ACT FOR YOUR BENEFIT AND IN ACCORDANCE WITH THE PROVISIONS OF THIS FORM AND MUST KEEP A RECORD OF RECEIPTS, DISBURSEMENTS, AND SIGNIFICANT ACTIONS TAKEN AS AGENT. YOU MAY NAME SUCCESSOR AGENTS UNDER THIS FORM BUT NOT CO-AGENTS. UNTIL YOU REVOKE THIS POWER OF ATTORNEY OR A COURT ACTING ON YOUR BEHALF TERMINATES IT, YOUR AGENT MAY EXERCISE THE POWERS GIVEN HERE THROUGHOUT YOUR LIFETIME, EVEN AFTER YOU MAY BECOME DISABLED, UNLESS YOU EXPRESSLY LIMIT THE DURATION OF THIS POWER IN THE MANNER PROVIDED BELOW.

YOU MAY HAVE OTHER RIGHTS OR POWERS UNDER COLORADO LAW NOT SPECIFIED IN THIS FORM.

I, _____, (insert your full name and address), appoint _____ (insert the full name and address of the person appointed) as my agent (attorney-in-fact) to act for me in any lawful way with respect to the following initialed subjects:
TO GRANT ONE OR MORE OF THE FOLLOWING POWERS, INITIAL THE LINE IN FRONT OF EACH POWER YOU ARE GRANTING. TO WITHHOLD A POWER, DO NOT INITIAL THE LINE IN FRONT OF IT. YOU MAY, BUT NEED NOT, CROSS OUT EACH POWER WITHHELD.
INITIAL

___ (A) Real property transactions (when properly recorded).
___ (B) Tangible personal property transactions.
___ (C) Stock and bond transactions.
___ (D) Commodity and option transactions.
___ (E) Banking and other financial institution transactions.
___ (F) Business operating transactions.
___ (G) Insurance and annuity transactions.
___ (H) Estate, trust, and other beneficiary transactions.
___ (I) Claims and litigation.
___ (J) Personal and family maintenance.
___ (K) Benefits from social security, medicare, medicaid, or other governmental programs or military service.
___ (L) Retirement plan transactions.
___ (M) Tax matters.

UNLESS YOU DIRECT OTHERWISE, THIS POWER OF ATTORNEY IS EFFECTIVE IMMEDIATELY AND WILL CONTINUE UNTIL IT IS REVOKED OR TERMINATED AS SPECIFIED BELOW. STRIKE THROUGH AND WRITE YOUR INITIALS TO THE LEFT OF THE FOLLOWING SENTENCE IF YOU DO NOT WANT THIS POWER OF ATTORNEY TO CONTINUE IF YOU BECOME DISABLED, INCAPACITATED, OR INCOMPETENT.

1. This power of attorney will continue to be effective even though I become disabled, incapacitated, or incompetent.

YOU MAY INCLUDE ADDITIONS TO AND LIMITATIONS ON THE AGENT'S POWERS IN THIS POWER OF IF THEY ARE SPECIFICALLY DESCRIBED BELOW.

2. The powers granted above shall not include the following powers or shall be modified or limited in the following manner (here you may include any specific limitations you deem appropriate, such as a prohibition of or conditions on the sale of particular stock or real estate or special rules regarding borrowing by the agent):

3. In addition to the powers granted above, I grant my agent the following powers (here you may add any other delegable powers, such as the power to make gifts, exercise powers of appointment, name or change beneficiaries or joint tenants, or revoke or amend any trust specifically referred to below):

4. SPECIAL INSTRUCTIONS. ON THE FOLLOWING LINES YOU MAY GIVE SPECIAL INSTRUCTIONS TO YOUR AGENT:

YOUR AGENT WILL BE ENTITLED TO REIMBURSEMENT FOR ALL REASONABLE EXPENSES INCURRED IN ACTING UNDER THIS POWER OF ATTORNEY. STRIKE THROUGH AND INITIAL THE NEXT SENTENCE IF YOU DO NOT WANT YOUR AGENT TO ALSO BE ENTITLED TO REASONABLE COMPENSATION FOR SERVICES AS AGENT.

5. My agent is entitled to reasonable compensation for services rendered as agent under this power of attorney.

THIS POWER OF ATTORNEY MAY BE AMENDED IN ANY MANNER OR REVOKED BY YOU AT ANY TIME. ABSENT AMENDMENT OR REVOCATION, THE AUTHORITY GRANTED IN THIS POWER OF ATTORNEY IS EFFECTIVE WHEN THIS POWER OF ATTORNEY IS SIGNED AND CONTINUES IN EFFECT

UNTIL YOUR DEATH, UNLESS YOU MAKE A LIMITATION ON DURATION BY COMPLETING THE FOLLOWING:

6. This power of attorney terminates on _____ (Insert a future date or event, such as court determination of your disability, when you want this power to terminate prior to your death).

BY RETAINING THE FOLLOWING PARAGRAPH, YOU MAY, BUT ARE NOT REQUIRED TO, NAME YOUR AGENT AS GUARDIAN OF YOUR PERSON OR CONSERVATOR OF YOUR PROPERTY, OR BOTH, IF A COURT PROCEEDING IS BEGUN TO APPOINT A GUARDIAN OR CONSERVATOR, OR BOTH, FOR YOU. THE COURT WILL APPOINT YOUR AGENT AS GUARDIAN OR CONSERVATOR, OR BOTH, IF THE COURT FINDS THAT SUCH APPOINTMENT WILL SERVE YOUR BEST INTERESTS AND WELFARE. STRIKE THROUGH AND INITIAL PARAGRAPH 7 IF YOU DO NOT WANT YOUR AGENT TO ACT AS GUARDIAN OR CONSERVATOR, OR BOTH.

7. If a guardian of my person or a conservator for my property, or both, are to be appointed, I nominate the agent acting under this power of attorney as such guardian or conservator, or both, to serve without bond or security.

IF YOU WISH TO NAME SUCCESSOR AGENTS, INSERT THE NAME AND ADDRESS OF ANY SUCCESSOR AGENT IN THE FOLLOWING PARAGRAPH:

8. If any agent named by me shall die, become incapacitated, resign, or refuse to accept the office of agent, I name the following each to act alone and successively, in the order named, as successor to such agent:

For purposes of this paragraph 8, a person is considered to be incapacitated if and while the person is a minor or a person adjudicated incapacitated or if the person is unable to give prompt and intelligent consideration to business matters, as certified by a licensed physician.

I agree that any third party who receives a copy of this document may act under it. Revocation of the power of attorney is not effective as to a third party until the third party learns of the revocation. I agree to indemnify the third party for any claims that arise against the third party because of reliance on this power of attorney.

Signed on _____, 20____.

IF THERE IS ANYTHING ABOUT THIS FORM THAT YOU DO NOT UNDER-STAND, IT MAY BE IN YOUR BEST INTEREST TO CONSULT A COLORADO LAWYER RATHER THAN SIGN THIS FORM.

_____
(Your Signature)

_____
(Your Social Security Number)

YOU MAY, BUT ARE NOT REQUIRED TO, REQUEST YOUR AGENT AND SUCCESSOR AGENTS TO PROVIDE SPECIMEN SIGNATURES BELOW. IF YOU INCLUDE SPECIMEN SIGNATURES IN THIS POWER OF ATTORNEY, YOU MUST COMPLETE THE CERTIFICATION OPPOSITE THE SIGNATURES OF THE AGENTS.

NOTICE TO AGENTS: BY EXERCISING POWERS UNDER THIS DOCUMENT, THE AGENT ASSUMES THE FIDUCIARY AND OTHER LEGAL RESPONSIBILITIES OF AN AGENT UNDER COLORADO LAW.

Specimen signatures of agent (and successors)

I certify that the signatures (and successors) of my agent (and successors) are correct.

_____   _____
Agent   Principal

_____   _____
Successor Agent   Principal

_____   _____
Successor Agent Principal

STATE OF COLORADO   )
) ss.
County of _____)

This document was acknowledged before me on _____ (date) by _____ (name of principal) who certifies the correctness of the signature(s) of the agent(s).
My commission expires: _____.

[Seal]
_____
Notary Public

(2) Requirements. A statutory power of attorney is legally sufficient under this act, if the wording of the form complies substantially with subsection (1), the form is properly completed, and the signature of the principal is acknowledged.

COLORADO REVISED STATUTES
TITLE 15
PROBATE, TRUSTS, AND FIDUCIARIES
ARTICLE 11
SUCCESSION AND WILLS*

5-11-502. Execution - witnessed or notarized wills - holographic wills. (1) Except as otherwise provided in subsection (2) of this section and in sections 15-11-503, 15-11-506, and 15-11-513, a will shall be:

(a) In writing;

(b) Signed by the testator, or in the testator's name by some other individual in the testator's conscious presence and by the testator's direction; and

(c) Either:

(I) Signed by at least two individuals, either prior to or after the testator's death, each of whom signed within a reasonable time after he or she witnessed either the testator's signing of the will as described in paragraph (b) of this subsection (1) or the testator's acknowledgment of that signature or acknowledgment of the will; OR

(II) Acknowledged by the Testator before a Notary Public or other individual authorized by law to take acknowledgments

15-11-504. Self-proved will.

(1) A will that is executed with attesting witnesses may be simultaneously executed, attested, and made self-proved by acknowledgment thereof by the testator and affidavits of the witnesses, each made before an officer authorized to administer oaths under the laws of the state in which execution occurs and evidenced by the officer's certificate, under official seal, in substantially the following form:

I, _____, the testator, sign my name to this instrument this _____ day of _____, and being first duly sworn, do hereby declare to the undersigned authority that I sign and execute this instrument as my will and that I sign it willingly (or willingly direct another to sign for me), that I execute it as my free and voluntary act for the purposes therein expressed, and that I am eighteen years of age or older, of sound mind, and under no constraint or undue influence.

_____
Testator

We, _____, _____ the witnesses, sign our names to this instrument, being first duly sworn, and do hereby declare to the undersigned authority that the testator signs and executes this instrument as [his] [her] will and that [he] [she] signs it willingly (or willingly directs another to sign for [him] [her]), and that [he] [she] executes it as [his] [her] free and voluntary act for the purposes therein expressed, and that each of us, in the conscious presence of the testator, hereby signs this will as witness to the testator's signing, and that to the best of our knowledge the testator is eighteen years of age or older, of sound mind, and under no constraint or undue influence.

_____
Witness

_____
Witness

THE STATE OF _____
COUNTY OF _____

Subscribed, sworn to and acknowledged before me by _____, the testator, and subscribed and sworn to before me by _____ and _____, witnesses, this _____ day of _____, ____.
(SEAL) (SIGNED)_____

_____
(Official capacity of officer)

(2) An attested A will that is executed with attesting witnesses may be made self-proved at any time after its execution by the acknowledgment thereof by the testator and the affidavits of the witnesses, each made before an officer authorized to administer oaths under the laws of the state in which the acknowledgment occurs and evidenced by the officer's certificate, under the official seal, attached or annexed to the will in substantially the following form:

THE STATE OF _____
COUNTY OF _____

We, _____, _____, and _____, the testator and the witnesses, respectively, whose names are signed to the attached or foregoing instrument, being first duly sworn, do hereby declare to the undersigned authority that the testator signed and executed the instrument as the testator's will and that [he] [she] had signed willingly (or willingly directed another to sign for [him] [her]), and that [he] [she] executed it as [his] [her] free and voluntary act for the purposes therein expressed, and that each of the witnesses, in the conscious presence of the testator, signed the will as witness and that to the best of [his] [her] knowledge the testator was at that time eighteen years of age or older, of sound mind, and under no constraint or undue influence.

_____
Testator

_____
Witness

_____
Witness

Subscribed, sworn to, and acknowledged before me by _____, the testator, and subscribed and sworn to before me by _____ and _____, witnesses, this _____ day of _____, _____.
(SEAL) (SIGNED)_____

_____
(Official capacity of officer)

(3) A signature affixed to a self-proving affidavit attached to a will is considered a signature affixed to the will if necessary to prove the will's due execution.

TITLE 18
CRIMINAL CODE
ARTICLE 8
GOVERNMENTAL OPERATIONS

18-8-404. First degree official misconduct.

(1) A public servant commits first degree official misconduct if, with intent to obtain a benefit for the public servant or another or maliciously to cause harm to another, he or she knowingly:

(a) Commits an act relating to his office but constituting an unauthorized exercise of his official function; or

(b) Refrains from performing a duty imposed upon him by law; or

(c) Violates any statute or lawfully adopted rule or regulation relating to his office.

(2) First degree official misconduct is a class 2 misdemeanor.

TITLE 24
GOVERNMENT — STATE
ARTICLE 4
RULE-MAKING AND LICENSING PROCEDURES BY STATE AGENCIES

24-4-105 (7) (15). Hearings and Determinations.

(7) Except as otherwise provided by statute, the proponent of an order shall have the burden of proof, and every party to the proceeding shall have the right to present his case or defense by oral and documentary evidence, to submit rebuttal evidence, and to conduct such cross-examination as may be required for a full and true disclosure of the facts. Subject to these rights and requirements, where a hearing will be expedited and the interests of the parties will not be substantially prejudiced thereby, a person conducting a hearing may receive all or part of the evidence in written form. The rules of evidence and requirements of proof shall conform, to the extent practicable, with those in civil nonjury cases in the district courts. However, when necessary to do so in order to ascertain facts affecting the substantial rights of the parties to the proceeding, the person so conducting the hearing may receive and consider evidence not admissible under such rules if such evidence possesses probative value commonly accepted by reasonable and prudent men in the conduct of their affairs. Objections to evidentiary offers may be made and shall be noted in the record. The person conducting a hearing shall give effect to the rules of privilege recognized by law. He may exclude incompetent and unduly repetitious evidence.

Documentary evidence may be received in the form of a copy or excerpt if the original is not readily available; but, upon request, the party shall be given an opportunity to compare the copy with the original. An agency may utilize its experience, technical competence, and specialized knowledge in the evaluation of the evidence presented to it.

(15)(a) Any party who seeks to reverse or modify the initial decision of the administrative law judge or the hearing officer shall file with the agency, within twenty days following such decision, a designation of the relevant parts of the record described in subsection (14) of this section and of the parts of the transcript of the proceedings which shall be prepared and advance the cost therefor. A copy of this designation shall be served on all parties. Within ten days thereafter, any other party or the agency may also file a designation of additional parts of the transcript of the proceedings which is to be included and advance the cost therefor. The transcript or the parts thereof which may be designated by the parties or the agency shall be prepared by the reporter or, in the case of an electronic recording device, the agency and shall thereafter be filed with the agency. No transcription is required if the agency's review is limited to a pure question of law. The agency may permit oral argument. The grounds of the decision shall be within the scope of the issues presented on the record. The record shall include all matters constituting the record upon which the decision of the administrative law judge or the hearing officer was based, the rulings upon the proposed findings and conclusions, the initial decision of the administrative law judge or the hearing officer, and any other exceptions and briefs filed.

(b) The findings of evidentiary fact, as distinguished from ultimate conclusions of fact, made by the administrative law judge or the hearing officer shall not be set aside by the agency on review of the initial decision unless such findings of evidentiary fact are contrary to the weight of the evidence. The agency may remand the case to the administrative law judge or the hearing officer for such further proceedings as it may direct, or it may affirm, set aside, or modify the order or any sanction or relief entered therein, in conformity with the facts and the law.

TITLE 38
PROPERTY — REAL AND PERSONAL
ARTICLE 30
TITLES TO MANUFACTURED HOMES

38-30-136. Subsequent proof of execution — proof or acknowledgment of copy.

(1) When any deed or instrument of writing has been executed and not acknowledged according to law at the time of the execution thereof, such deed or instrument of writing may at any subsequent time be acknowledged by the makers thereof in the manner provided in this article, or proof may be made of the execution thereof before any officer authorized to take acknowledgments of deeds in the manner provided in this section. Such officer, when the fact is not within his own knowledge, shall ascertain from the testimony of at least one competent, credible witness, to be sworn and examined by him, that the person offering to prove the execution of such deed or writing is a subscribing witness thereto. Thereupon such officer shall examine such subscribing witness upon oath or affirmation, and shall reduce his testimony to writing and require the witness to subscribe the same, endorsed upon or attached to such deed or other writing, and shall thereupon grant a certificate that such witness was personally known or was proved to him by the testimony of at least one witness (who shall be named in such certificate) to be a subscribing witness to the deed or instrument of writing to be proved, that such subscribing witness was lawfully sworn and examined by him, and that the testimony of the said officer was reduced to writing and by said subscribing witness subscribed in his presence.

(2) If by the testimony it appears that such witness saw the person, whose name is subscribed to such instrument of writing, sign, seal, and deliver the same or that such person afterwards acknowledged the same to the said witness to be his free and voluntary act or deed and that such witness subscribed the said deed or instrument of writing in attestation thereof, in the presence and with the consent of the person so executing the same, such proof if attested and the authority of the officer to take the same duly proved in the same manner as required in the case of acknowledgment, shall have the same force and effect as an acknowledgment of said deed or instrument of writing by the person executing the same, and duly certified.

(3) When any such deed or instrument of writing has been executed and recorded without due proof, attestation or acknowledgment as required by law, a certified copy from such record may be proved or acknowledged in the same manner and with like effect as the original thereof. No person shall be permitted to use such certified copy so proved as evidence except upon satisfactory proof that the original thereof has been lost or destroyed or is beyond his power to produce.

38-35-101. Acknowledgments — form — prima facie evidence.

(1) No officer authorized to take acknowledgments of instruments affecting title to real property shall take or certify such acknowledgments unless the person making the same is personally known to such officer to be the identical person he represents himself to be or is proved to be such by at least one credible person known to such officer. It shall not be necessary to state such fact in his certificate of acknowledgment attached to any instrument affecting title to real property.

(2) Any deed or other instrument relating to or affecting title to real property acknowledged substantially in accordance with the following form before a proper official shall be prima facie evidence of the proper execution thereof:

STATE OF COLORADO)
) ss.
County of _____)

The foregoing instrument was acknowledged before me this _____ day of _____, 20___, by _____ _____ _____ (if by natural person or persons, insert name or names; if by person acting in representative or official capacity or as attorney-in-fact, insert name of person as executor, attorney-in-fact, or other capacity or description; if by officer of corporation, insert name of such officer or officers as the president or other officers of such corporation, naming it). If acknowledgment is taken by a notary public, the date of expiration of his commission shall also appear on the certificate.

Witness my hand and official seal.

Title of Officer

TITLE 1
ELECTIONS
ARTICLE 1
ELECTIONS GENERALLY

1-1-104 (19.5) (b) "Identification" means:

(I) A valid Colorado driver's license;

(II) A valid identification card issued by the department of revenue in accordance with the requirements of part 3 of article 2 of title 42, C.R.S.;

(III) A valid United States passport;

(IV) A valid employee identification card with a photograph of the eligible elector issued by any branch, department, agency, or entity of the United States government or of this state, or by any county, municipality, board, authority, or other political subdivision of this state;

(V) A valid pilot's license issued by the federal aviation administration or other authorized agency of the United States;

(VI) A valid United States military identification card with a photograph of the eligible elector;

(VII) A copy of a current utility bill, bank statement, government check, paycheck, or other government document that shows the name and address of the elector;

(VIII) A valid medicare or medicaid card issued by the United States health care financing administration;

(IX) A certified copy of a birth certificate for the elector issued in the United States;

(X) Certified documentation of naturalization; or

(XI) A valid student identification card with a photograph of the eligible elector issued by an institution of higher education in Colorado, as defined in section 23-3.1-102 (5), C.R.S.

(b) Any form of identification indicated in paragraph (a) of this subsection (19.5) that shows the address of the eligible elector shall be considered identification only if the address is in the state of Colorado.

TITLE 1
ELECTIONS
ARTICLE 40
INITIATIVE AND REFERENDUM

1-40-101. Legislative declaration. (1) THE GENERAL ASSEMBLY DECLARES THAT it is not the intention of this article to limit or abridge in any manner the powers reserved to the people in the initiative and referendum, but rather to properly safeguard, protect, and preserve inviolate for them these modern instrumentalities of democratic government.

(2) (a) The general assembly finds, determines, and declares that:

(i) The initiative process relies upon the truthfulness of circulators who obtain the petition signatures to qualify a ballot issue for the statewide ballot and that during the 2008 general election, the honesty of many petition circulators was at issue because of practices that included: using third parties to circulate petition sections, even though the third parties did not sign the circulator's affidavit, were not of legal age to act as a circulator, and were paid in cash to conceal their identities; providing false names or residential addresses in the circulator's affidavits, a practice that permits circulators to evade detection by persons challenging the secretary of state's sufficiency determination; circulating petition sections without even a rudimentary understanding of the legal requirements relating to petition circulation; and obtaining the signatures of persons who purported to notarize circulator affidavits, even though such persons were not legally authorized to act as notaries or administer the required oath;

(ii) The per signature compensation system used by many petition entities provides an incentive for circulators to collect as many signatures as possible, without regard for whether all petition signers are registered electors; and

(iii) Many petition circulator affidavits are thus executed without regard for specific requirements of law that are designed to assist in the prevention of fraud, abuse, and mistake in the initiative process.

(b) The general assembly further finds, determines, and declares that:

(i) because petition circulators who reside in other states typically leave Colorado immediately after petitions are submitted to the secretary of state for verification, a full and fair examination of fraud related to petition circulation is frustrated, and as a result, the secretary of state has been forced to give effect to certain circulator affidavits that were not properly verified and thus were not prima facie evidence of the validity of petition signatures on affected petition sections; and

(ii) The courts have not had authority to exercise jurisdiction over fraudulent acts by circulators and notaries public in connection with petition signatures reviewed as part of the secretary of state's random sample.

(c) Therefore, the general assembly finds, determines, and declares that:

(i) As a result of the problems identified in paragraphs (a) and (a) of this subsection (2), one or more ballot measures appeared on the statewide ballot at the 2008 general election even though significant numbers of the underlying petition signatures were obtained in direct violation of Colorado law and the accuracy of the secretary of state's determination of sufficiency could not be fully evaluated by the district court; and

(ii) For the initiative process to operate as an honest expression of the voters' reserved legislative power, it is essential that circulators truthfully verify all elements of their circulator affidavits and make themselves available to participate in challenges to the secretary of state's determination of petition sufficiency.

1-40-102. Definitions. As used in this article, unless the context otherwise requires:

(3.5) "Circulator" means a person who presents to other persons for possible signature a petition to place a measure on the ballot by initiative or referendum.

***

1-40-111. Signatures - affidavits - notarization - list of circulators and notaries.

***

(2) (a) To each petition section shall be attached a signed, notarized, and dated affidavit executed by the person who circulated the petition section, which shall include his or her printed name, the address at which he or she resides, including the street name and number, the city or town, the county, and the date he or she signed the affidavit; that he or she has read and understands the laws governing the circulation of petitions; that he or she was a resident of the state, a citizen of the United States, and at least eighteen years of age at the time the section of the petition was circulated and signed by the listed electors; that he or she circulated the section of the petition; that each signature thereon was affixed in the circulator's presence; that each signature thereon is the signature of the person whose name it purports to be; that to the best of the circulator's knowledge and belief each of the persons signing the petition section was, at the time of signing, a registered elector; and that he or she has not paid or will not in the future pay and that he or she believes that no other person has paid or will pay, directly or indirectly, any money or other thing of value to any signer for the purpose of inducing or causing such signer to affix his or her signature to the petition; that he or she understands that he or she can be prosecuted for violating the laws governing the circulation of petitions, including the requirement that a circulator truthfully completed the affidavit and that each signature thereon was affixed in the circulator's presence; and that he or she understands that failing to make himself or herself available to be deposed and to provide testimony in the event of a protest shall invalidate the petition section if it is challenged on the grounds of circulator fraud.

(b) (i) A notary public shall not notarize an affidavit required pursuant to paragraph (a) of this subsection (2), unless:

(A) The circulator is in the physical presence of the notary public;

(B) The circulator has dated the affidavit and fully and accurately completed all of the personal information on the affidavit required pursuant to paragraph (A) of this subsection (2); and

(C) The circulator presents a form of identification, as such term is defined in section 1-1-104 (19.5). A notary public shall specify the form of identification presented to him or her on a blank line, which shall be part of the affidavit form.

(ii) An affidavit that is notarized in violation of any provision of subparagraph (i) of this paragraph (b) shall be invalid.

(iii) If the date signed by a circulator on an affidavit required pursuant to paragraph (a) of this subsection (2) is different from the date signed by the notary public, the affidavit shall be invalid. If, notwithstanding sub-subparagraph (B) of subparagraph (i) of this paragraph (b), a notary public notarizes an affidavit that has not been dated by the circulator, the notarization date shall not cure the circulator's failure to sign the affidavit and the affidavit shall be invalid.

(c) The secretary of state shall not accept for filing reject any section of a petition that does not have attached thereto the a valid notarized affidavit required by this section that complies with all of the requirements set forth in paragraphs (a) and (b) of this subsection (2). Any signature added to a section of a petition after the affidavit has been executed shall be invalid.

(3) (a) As part of any court proceeding or hearing conducted by the secretary of state related to a protest of all or part of a petition section, the circulator of such petition section shall be required to make himself or herself available to be deposed and to testify in person, by telephone, or by any other means permitted under the Colorado Rules of Civil Procedure. Except as set forth in paragraph (b) of this subsection (3), the petition section that is the subject of the protest shall be invalid if a circulator fails to comply with the requirement set forth in this paragraph (a) for any protest that includes an allegation of circulator fraud that is plead with particularity regarding:

(i) Forgery of a registered elector's signature;

(ii) Circulation of a petition section, in whole or part, by anyone other than the person who signs the affidavit attached to the petition section;

(iii) Use of a false circulator name or address in the affidavit; or

(iv) Payment of money or other things of value to any person for the purpose of inducing the person to sign the petition.

(b) Upon the finding by a district court or the secretary of state that the circulator of a petition section is unable to be deposed or to testify at trial or a hearing conducted by the secretary of state because the circulator has died, become mentally incompetent, or become medically incapacitated and physically unable to testify by any means whatsoever, the provisions of paragraph (a) of this subsection (3) shall not apply to invalidate a petition section circulated by the circulator.

(4) The proponents of a petition or an issue committee acting on the proponents' behalf shall maintain a list of the names and addresses of all circulators who circulated petition sections on behalf of the proponents and notaries public who notarized petition sections on behalf of the proponents and the petition section numbers that each circulator circulated and that each notary public notarized. A copy of the list shall be filed with the secretary of state along with the petition. If a copy of the list is not filed, the secretary of state shall prepare the list and charge the proponents a fee, which shall be determined and collected pursuant to section 24-21-104 (3), C.R.S., to cover the cost of the preparation. Once filed or prepared by the secretary of state, the list shall be a public record for purposes of article 72 of title 24, C.R.S.

***

1-40-112. Circulators - requirements - training - rules.

(3) The secretary of state shall develop circulator training programs for paid and volunteer circulators. Such programs shall be conducted in the broadest, most

cost-effective manner available to the secretary of state, including but not limited to training sessions for persons associated with the proponents or a petition entity, as defined in section 1-40-135 (1), and by electronic and remote access. The proponents of an initiative petition or the representatives of a petition entity shall inform paid and volunteer circulators of the availability of these training programs as one manner of complying with the requirement set forth in the circulator's affidavit that a circulator read and understand the laws pertaining to petition circulation.

(4) It shall be unlawful for any person to pay a circulator more than twenty percent of his or her compensation for circulating petitions on a per signature or petition section basis.

***

1-40-118. Protest. (1) A protest in writing, under oath, together with three copies thereof, may be filed in the district court for the county in which the petition has been filed by some registered elector, within thirty days after the secretary of state issues a statement as to whether the petition has a sufficient number of valid signatures, which statement shall be issued no later than thirty calendar days after the petition has been filed. If the secretary of state fails to issue a statement within thirty calendar days, the petition shall be deemed sufficient. Regardless of whether the secretary of state has issued a statement of sufficiency or if the petition is deemed sufficient because the secretary of state has failed to issue a statement of sufficiency within thirty calendar days, no further agency action shall be necessary for the district court to have jurisdiction to consider the protest. During the period a petition is being examined by the secretary of state for sufficiency, the petition shall not be available to the public; except that such period shall not exceed thirty calendar days. Immediately after the secretary of state issues a statement of sufficiency or, if the petition is deemed sufficient because the secretary of state has failed to issue the statement, after thirty calendar days, the secretary of state shall make the petition available to the public for copying upon request.

***

(2.5) (a) If a district court finds that there are invalid signatures or petition sections as a result of fraud committed by any person involved in petition circulation, the registered elector who instituted the proceedings may commence a civil action to recover reasonable attorney fees and costs from the person responsible for such invalid signatures or petition sections.

***

(5) Written entries that are made by petition signers, circulators, and notaries public on a petition section that substantially comply with the requirements of this article shall be deemed valid by the secretary of state or any court, unless:

(a) Fraud, as specified in section 1-40-135 (2) (c), excluding subparagraph (v) of said paragraph (c), is established by a preponderance of the evidence;

(b) A violation of any provision of this article or any other provision of law that, in either case, prevents fraud, abuse, or mistake in the petition process, is established by a preponderance of the evidence;

(c) A circulator used a petition form that does not comply with the provisions of this article or has not been approved by the secretary of state.

***

1-40-130. Unlawful acts - penalty. (1) It is unlawful:

(h) For any officer or person to violate willfully any provision of this article. article;

(i) For any person to pay money or other things of value to a registered elector for the purpose of inducing the elector to withdraw his or her name from a petition for a ballot issue;

(j) For any person to certify an affidavit attached to a petition in violation of section 1-40-111 (2) (b) (i);

(k) for any person to sign any affidavit as a circulator, unless each signature in the petition section to which the affidavit is attached was affixed in the presence of the circulator;

(l) For any person to circulate in whole or in part a petition section, unless such person is the circulator who signs the affidavit attached to the petition section.

(2) Any person, upon conviction of a violation of any provision of this section, shall be punished by a fine of not more than one thousand five hundred dollars, or by imprisonment for not more than one year in the county jail, or by both such fine and imprisonment.

***

1-40-135. Petition entities - requirements - definitions.

(1) As used in this section, "petition entity" means any person or issue committee that provides compensation to a circulator to circulate a ballot petition.

(2) (a) It is unlawful for any petition entity to provide compensation to a circulator to circulate a petition without first obtaining a license therefor from the secretary of state. The secretary of state may deny a license if he or she finds that the petition entity or any of its principals have been found, in a judicial or administrative proceeding, to have violated the petition laws of Colorado or any other state and such violation involves authorizing or knowingly permitting any of the acts set forth in paragraph (c) of this subsection (2), excluding subparagraph (v) of said paragraph (c). the secretary of state shall deny a license:

(i) Unless the petition entity agrees that it shall not pay a circulator more than twenty percent of his or her compensation on a per signature or per petition basis; or

(ii) If no current representative of the petition entity has completed the training related to potential fraudulent activities in petition circulation, as established by the secretary of state, pursuant to section 1-40-112 (3).

(b) The secretary of state may at any time request the petition entity to provide documentation that demonstrates compliance with section 1-40-112 (4).

(c) The secretary of state shall revoke the petition entity license if, at any time after receiving a license, a petition entity is determined to no longer be in compliance with the requirements set forth in paragraph (a) of this subsection (2) or if the petition entity authorized or knowingly permitted:

(i) Forgery of a registered elector's signature;

(ii) Circulation of a petition section, in whole or part, by anyone other than the circulator who signs the affidavit attached to the petition section;

(iii) Use of a false circulator name or address in the affidavit;

(iv) Payment of money or other things of value to any person for the purpose of inducing the person to sign or withdraw his or her name from the petition;

(v) Payment to a circulator of more than twenty percent of his or her compensation on a per signature or per petition section basis; or

(vi) A notary public's notarization of a petition section outside of the presence of the circulator or without the production of the required identification for notarization of a petition section.

CODE OF COLORADO REGULATIONS

Title 8 Department of State
Chapter 1505-11 Notary Program Rules
Rule 1. Definitions

1.1 "Approved course of instruction" means a live classroom or webcast course approved by the Secretary of State.

1.2 "Approved vendor" means a vendor approved by the Secretary of State who provides an approved course of instruction to notaries and prospective notaries for a fee.

1.3 "Course provider" means an entity other than an individual that uses the Secretary of State's curriculum, in addition to any entity-specific practices, to provide notary training to its employees or members free of charge.

1.4 "DAN" means the unique document authentication number issued by the Secretary of State and required by sections 12-55-106.5, 12-55-111(4), and 12-55-112(4.5)(b), C.R.S., for electronic notarizations.

1.5 "Electronic notarization" means a notary's notarization of electronic records that includes the notary's and the document signer's electronic signatures.

1.6 "Electronic notarization software" means any software, coding, disk, card, certificate, or program that creates and affixes the notary's electronic signature.

1.7 "New applicant" means a person seeking a commission as a Colorado notary for the first time or a formerly commissioned notary in Colorado whose commission has been expired for more than 30 days.

Rule 2. Notary Commissions

2.1 Filing and training requirements

2.1.1 All notary filings must be submitted via the Secretary of State's online electronic filing system.

2.1.2 No more than six months before applying for a commission, a new applicant must successfully complete training and pass the exam administered by the Secretary of State.

2.1.3 The Secretary of State will grant credit only for completion of courses offered by an approved vendor, an approved course provider, or the Secretary of State.

2.1.4 The Secretary of State may require a notary who has committed misconduct meriting a disciplinary proceeding to retake and successfully complete the training and exam.

2.1.5 Examination. The Secretary of State's open book examination will test the applicant's understanding of notary duties contained in the following:

(a) Title 12, Article 55 (The Notaries Public Act) of the Colorado Revised Statutes;

(b) Title 38, Article 30 (Titles and Interests) of the Colorado Revised Statutes;

(c) Title 1, Article 40 (Initiative and Referendum) of the Colorado Revised Statutes; and

(d) The Official Notary Handbook published by the Secretary of State.

2.2 Electronic notarization

2.2.1 A notary must submit a notice of intent on the approved form and receive approval from the Secretary of State before the notary may electronically notarize a document. A new applicant may file the intent at the time of application but may only electronically notarize a document after he or she has been commissioned and approved. If the applicant intends to use a different electronic signature than a DAN, the applicant must attach an example of the electronic signature, a description of the electronic signature technology, and contact information for the technology's supplier or vendor. A notary must notify the Secretary of State of all electronic signature changes.

2.2.2 A notary must include his or her notary identification number in an electronic notarization.

2.2.3 For purposes of section 12-55-106.5(1), C.R.S., a notary's name means the notary's printed legal name.

2.2.4 A notary must:

(a) Use a different DAN for each electronic notarization;

(b) Take reasonable measures to secure assigned DANs against another person's access or use and must not permit such access or use; and

(c) Request new DANs to replace lost or stolen DANs after notifying the Secretary in the same manner as for a journal or seal.

2.2.5 A notary must verify that the document signer has adopted an electronic signature to function as his or her signature before electronically notarizing a document.

2.2.6 Expiration of the Secretary of State's approval to notarize electronically

(a) Approval automatically expires:

(1) Upon revocation, expiration, or resignation of the notary's commission;

(2) 30 days after the notary's name changes unless the notary previously submitted a name change.

(3) Upon conviction of a felony;

(4) If the notary moves out of Colorado; or

(5) Upon the expiration or revocation of the technology described in the notification.

(b) If approval expires, the notary or the notary's authorized representative must destroy all electronic notarization software and unused DANs unless:

(1) The notary's commission expired; and

(2) Within 30 days of the commission's expiration, the Secretary of State recommissions the notary and the notary reregisters his or her electronic signature.

SENATE BILL 20-096

BY SENATOR(S) Rodriguez and Holbert, Bridges, Fields, Ginal, Lee, Marble, Priola, Smallwood, Sonnenberg, Story, Tate, Todd, Williams A.; also REPRESENTATIVE(S) Duran and Carver, Arndt, Bird, Caraveo, Champion, Coleman, Cutter, Exum, Garnett, Gonzales-Gutierrez, Gray, Herod, Humphrey, Jackson, Jaquez Lewis, Kennedy, Kipp, Lontine, Melton, Michaelson Jenet, Ransom, Rich, Saine, Singer, Sirota, Snyder, Soper, Titone, Valdez A., Valdez D., Van Winkle, Young, Becker.

CONCERNING AN AUTHORIZATION FOR NOTARIES PUBLIC TO PERFORM NOTARIAL ACTS USING AUDIO-VIDEO COMMUNICATION, AND, IN CONNECTION THEREWITH, MAKING AN APPROPRIATION.

Be it enacted by the General Assembly of the State of Colorado:

SECTION 1. Legislative declaration. The general assembly recognizes the importance of protecting personal information that is disclosed and recorded, including both audio and video, during the remote notarization process. Data privacy is an essential part of Colorado's authorization of remote notarization and the security of personal data from unauthorized use or theft is of critical importance in the implementation of remote notarization requirements in Colorado.

Capital letters or bold & italic numbers indicate new material added to existing law; dashes through words or numbers indicate deletions from existing law and such material is not part of the act.

SECTION 2. In Colorado Revised Statutes, 24-21-502, **add** (1.3), (1.7), (10.5), (11.3), (11.5), (11.7), and (15.5) as follows:

24-21-502. Definitions. In this part 5:

(1.3) "AUDIO-VIDEO COMMUNICATION" MEANS COMMUNICATION BY WHICH AN INDIVIDUAL IS ABLE TO SEE, HEAR, AND COMMUNICATE WITH A REMOTELY LOCATED INDIVIDUAL IN REAL TIME USING ELECTRONIC MEANS.

(1.7) "CREDENTIAL" MEANS A TANGIBLE RECORD EVIDENCING THE IDENTITY OF AN INDIVIDUAL.

(10.5) "REAL-TIME" OR "IN REAL TIME" MEANS, WITH RESPECT TO AN INTERACTION BETWEEN INDIVIDUALS BY MEANS OF AUDIO-VIDEO COMMUNICATION, THAT THE INDIVIDUALS CAN SEE AND HEAR EACH OTHER SUBSTANTIALLY SIMULTANEOUSLY AND WITHOUT INTERRUPTION OR DISCONNECTION. DELAYS OF A FEW SECONDS THAT ARE INHERENT IN THE METHOD OF COMMUNICATION DO NOT PREVENT THE INTERACTION FROM BEING CONSIDERED TO HAVE OCCURRED IN REAL TIME.

(11.3) "REMOTELY LOCATED INDIVIDUAL" MEANS AN INDIVIDUAL WHO IS NOT IN THE PHYSICAL PRESENCE OF THE NOTARY PUBLIC WHO PERFORMS A NOTARIAL ACT UNDER THIS SECTION.

(11.5) "REMOTE NOTARIZATION" MEANS AN ELECTRONIC NOTARIAL ACT PERFORMED WITH RESPECT ONLY TO AN ELECTRONIC RECORD BY MEANS OF REAL-TIME AUDIO-VIDEO COMMUNICATION IN ACCORDANCE WITH SECTION 24-21-514.5 AND RULES ADOPTED BY THE SECRETARY OF STATE.

(11.7) "REMOTE NOTARIZATION SYSTEM" MEANS AN ELECTRONIC DEVICE OR PROCESS THAT:

(a) ALLOWS A NOTARY PUBLIC AND A REMOTELY LOCATED INDIVIDUAL TO COMMUNICATE WITH EACH OTHER SIMULTANEOUSLY BY SIGHT AND SOUND; AND

(b) WHEN NECESSARY AND CONSISTENT WITH OTHER APPLICABLE LAW, FACILITATES COMMUNICATION WITH A REMOTELY LOCATED INDIVIDUAL WHO HAS A VISION, HEARING, OR SPEECH IMPAIRMENT.

(15.5) "TAMPER-EVIDENT" MEANS THE USE OF A SET OF APPLICATIONS, PROGRAMS, HARDWARE, SOFTWARE, OR OTHER TECHNOLOGIES THAT WILL DISPLAY EVIDENCE OF ANY CHANGES MADE TO AN ELECTRONIC RECORD.

SECTION 3. In Colorado Revised Statutes, **amend** 24-21-506 as follows:

24-21-506. Personal appearance required - definition. (1) If a notarial act relates to a statement made in or a signature executed on a record, the individual making the statement or executing the signature shall appear personally before the notarial officer.

(2) FOR PURPOSES OF THIS SECTION, "APPEAR PERSONALLY" MEANS:

(a) BEING IN THE SAME PHYSICAL LOCATION AS ANOTHER INDIVIDUAL AND CLOSE ENOUGH TO SEE, HEAR, COMMUNICATE WITH, AND EXCHANGE TANGIBLE IDENTIFICATION CREDENTIALS WITH THAT INDIVIDUAL; OR

(b) INTERACTING WITH A REMOTELY LOCATED INDIVIDUAL BY MEANS OF REAL-TIME AUDIO-VIDEO COMMUNICATION IN COMPLIANCE WITH SECTION 24-21-514.5 AND RULES ADOPTED BY THE SECRETARY OF STATE.

SECTION 4. In Colorado Revised Statutes, **add** 24-21-514.5 as follows:

24-21-514.5. Audio-video communication - definitions. (1) AS USED IN THIS SECTION:

(a) "CREDENTIAL ANALYSIS" MEANS A PROCESS OR SERVICE THAT COMPLIES WITH ANY RULES ADOPTED BY THE SECRETARY OF STATE THROUGH WHICH A THIRD PARTY AFFIRMS THE VALIDITY OF A GOVERNMENT-ISSUED IDENTIFICATION CREDENTIAL THROUGH THE REVIEW OF PUBLIC OR PROPRIETARY DATA SOURCES.

(b) "DYNAMIC, KNOWLEDGE-BASED AUTHENTICATION ASSESSMENT" MEANS AN IDENTITY ASSESSMENT THAT IS BASED ON A SET OF QUESTIONS FORMULATED FROM PUBLIC OR PRIVATE DATA SOURCES FOR WHICH THE REMOTELY LOCATED INDIVIDUAL TAKING THE ASSESSMENT HAS NOT PREVIOUSLY PROVIDED AN ANSWER AND THAT MEETS ANY RULES ADOPTED BY THE SECRETARY OF STATE.

(c) "OUTSIDE THE UNITED STATES" MEANS A LOCATION OUTSIDE THE GEOGRAPHIC BOUNDARIES OF THE UNITED STATES, PUERTO RICO, THE UNITED STATES VIRGIN ISLANDS, AND ANY TERRITORY OR INSULAR POSSESSION SUBJECT TO THE JURISDICTION OF THE UNITED STATES.

(d) "PUBLIC KEY CERTIFICATE" MEANS AN ELECTRONIC CREDENTIAL THAT IS USED TO IDENTIFY A REMOTELY LOCATED INDIVIDUAL WHO SIGNED AN ELECTRONIC RECORD WITH THE CREDENTIAL.

(e) "REMOTE PRESENTATION" MEANS TRANSMISSION TO THE NOTARY PUBLIC THROUGH COMMUNICATION TECHNOLOGY OF AN IMAGE OF A

GOVERNMENT-ISSUED IDENTIFICATION CREDENTIAL THAT IS OF SUFFICIENT QUALITY TO ENABLE THE NOTARY PUBLIC TO:

(I) IDENTIFY THE REMOTELY LOCATED INDIVIDUAL SEEKING THE NOTARY PUBLIC'S SERVICES; AND

(II) PERFORM CREDENTIAL ANALYSIS.

(2) (a) EXCEPT AS PROVIDED IN SUBSECTION (2)(b) OF THIS SECTION, A NOTARY PUBLIC MAY PERFORM A REMOTE NOTARIZATION ONLY WITH RESPECT TO AN ELECTRONIC RECORD AND IN COMPLIANCE WITH THIS SECTION AND ANY RULES ADOPTED BY THE SECRETARY OF STATE FOR A REMOTELY LOCATED INDIVIDUAL WHO IS LOCATED:

(I) IN THIS STATE;

(II) OUTSIDE OF THIS STATE BUT WITHIN THE UNITED STATES; OR

(III) OUTSIDE THE UNITED STATES IF:

(A) THE NOTARY PUBLIC HAS NO ACTUAL KNOWLEDGE THAT THE NOTARIAL ACT IS PROHIBITED IN THE JURISDICTION IN WHICH THE REMOTELY LOCATED INDIVIDUAL IS PHYSICALLY LOCATED AT THE TIME OF THE ACT; AND

(B) THE REMOTELY LOCATED INDIVIDUAL CONFIRMS TO THE NOTARY PUBLIC THAT THE REQUESTED NOTARIAL ACT AND THE RECORD RELATE TO: A MATTER THAT WILL BE FILED WITH OR IS CURRENTLY BEFORE A COURT, GOVERNMENTAL ENTITY, OR OTHER ENTITY IN THE UNITED STATES; PROPERTY LOCATED IN THE UNITED STATES; OR A TRANSACTION SUBSTANTIALLY CONNECTED TO THE UNITED STATES.

(b) A NOTARY PUBLIC SHALL NOT USE A REMOTE NOTARIZATION SYSTEM TO NOTARIZE:

(I) A RECORD RELATING TO THE ELECTORAL PROCESS; OR

(II) A WILL, CODICIL, DOCUMENT PURPORTING TO BE A WILL OR CODICIL, OR ANY ACKNOWLEDGMENT REQUIRED UNDER SECTION 15-11-502 OR 15-11-504.

(3) BEFORE A NOTARY PUBLIC PERFORMS THE NOTARY PUBLIC'S INITIAL NOTARIZATION USING A REMOTE NOTARIZATION SYSTEM, THE NOTARY PUBLIC SHALL NOTIFY THE SECRETARY OF STATE THAT THE NOTARY PUBLIC WILL BE PERFORMING REMOTE NOTARIZATIONS AND SHALL IDENTIFY EACH REMOTE NOTARIZATION SYSTEM THAT THE NOTARY PUBLIC INTENDS TO USE. THE REMOTE NOTARIZATION SYSTEM MUST CONFORM TO THIS PART 5 AND ANY RULES ADOPTED BY THE SECRETARY OF STATE. THE NOTICE MUST BE SUBMITTED IN THE FORMAT REQUIRED BY THE SECRETARY OF STATE AND MUST:

(a) INCLUDE AN AFFIRMATION THAT THE NOTARY PUBLIC HAS READ AND WILL COMPLY WITH THIS SECTION AND ALL RULES ADOPTED BY THE SECRETARY OF STATE; AND

(b) BE ACCOMPANIED BY PROOF THAT THE NOTARY PUBLIC HAS SUCCESSFULLY COMPLETED ANY TRAINING AND EXAMINATION REQUIRED BY THE SECRETARY OF STATE.

(4) A NOTARY PUBLIC WHO PERFORMS A NOTARIAL ACT FOR A REMOTELY LOCATED INDIVIDUAL BY MEANS OF AUDIO-VIDEO COMMUNICATION MUST:

(a) BE LOCATED WITHIN THIS STATE AT THE TIME THE NOTARIAL ACT IS PERFORMED;

(b) EXECUTE THE NOTARIAL ACT IN A SINGLE, REAL-TIME SESSION;

(C) CONFIRM THAT ANY RECORD THAT IS SIGNED, ACKNOWLEDGED, OR OTHERWISE PRESENTED FOR NOTARIZATION BY THE REMOTELY LOCATED INDIVIDUAL IS THE SAME RECORD SIGNED BY THE NOTARY PUBLIC;

(d) CONFIRM THAT THE QUALITY OF THE AUDIO-VIDEO COMMUNICATION IS SUFFICIENT TO MAKE THE DETERMINATIONS REQUIRED FOR THE NOTARIAL ACT UNDER THIS PART 5 AND ANY OTHER LAW OF THIS STATE; AND

(e) IDENTIFY THE VENUE FOR THE NOTARIAL ACT AS THE JURISDICTION WITHIN THE STATE OF COLORADO WHERE THE NOTARY PUBLIC IS PHYSICALLY LOCATED WHILE PERFORMING THE ACT.

(5) A REMOTE NOTARIZATION SYSTEM USED TO PERFORM REMOTE NOTARIZATIONS MUST:

(a) REQUIRE THE NOTARY PUBLIC, THE REMOTELY LOCATED INDIVIDUAL, AND ANY REQUIRED WITNESS TO ACCESS THE SYSTEM THROUGH AN AUTHENTICATION PROCEDURE THAT COMPLIES WITH RULES ADOPTED BY THE SECRETARY OF STATE REGARDING SECURITY AND ACCESS;

(b) ENABLE THE NOTARY PUBLIC TO VERIFY THE IDENTITY OF THE REMOTELY LOCATED INDIVIDUAL AND ANY REQUIRED WITNESS BY MEANS OF PERSONAL KNOWLEDGE OR SATISFACTORY EVIDENCE OF IDENTITY IN COMPLIANCE WITH SUBSECTION (6) OF THIS SECTION; AND

(C) CONFIRM THAT THE NOTARY PUBLIC, THE REMOTELY LOCATED INDIVIDUAL, AND ANY REQUIRED WITNESS ARE VIEWING THE SAME RECORD AND THAT ALL SIGNATURES, CHANGES, AND ATTACHMENTS TO THE RECORD ARE MADE IN REAL TIME.

(6) (a) A NOTARY PUBLIC SHALL DETERMINE FROM PERSONAL KNOWLEDGE OR SATISFACTORY EVIDENCE OF IDENTITY AS DESCRIBED IN SUBSECTION (6) (b) OF THIS SECTION THAT THE REMOTELY LOCATED INDIVIDUAL APPEARING BEFORE THE NOTARY PUBLIC BY MEANS OF AUDIO-VIDEO COMMUNICATION IS THE INDIVIDUAL THAT HE OR SHE PURPORTS TO BE.

(b) A NOTARY PUBLIC HAS SATISFACTORY EVIDENCE OF IDENTITY IF THE NOTARY PUBLIC CAN IDENTIFY THE REMOTELY LOCATED INDIVIDUAL WHO PERSONALLY APPEARS BEFORE THE NOTARY PUBLIC BY MEANS OF AUDIO-VIDEO COMMUNICATION BY USING AT LEAST ONE OF THE FOLLOWING METHODS:

(I) THE OATH OR AFFIRMATION OF A CREDIBLE WITNESS WHO PERSONALLY KNOWS THE REMOTELY LOCATED INDIVIDUAL, IS PERSONALLY KNOWN TO THE NOTARY PUBLIC, AND IS IN THE PHYSICAL PRESENCE OF THE NOTARY PUBLIC OR THE REMOTELY LOCATED INDIVIDUAL DURING THE REMOTE NOTARIZATION;

(II) REMOTE PRESENTATION AND CREDENTIAL ANALYSIS OF A GOVERNMENT-ISSUED IDENTIFICATION CREDENTIAL, AND THE DATA CONTAINED ON THE CREDENTIAL, THAT CONTAINS THE SIGNATURE AND A PHOTOGRAPH OF THE REMOTELY LOCATED INDIVIDUAL, AND AT LEAST ONE OF THE FOLLOWING:

(A) A DYNAMIC, KNOWLEDGE-BASED AUTHENTICATION ASSESSMENT BY A TRUSTED THIRD PARTY THAT COMPLIES WITH RULES ADOPTED BY THE SECRETARY OF STATE;

(B) A VALID PUBLIC KEY CERTIFICATE THAT COMPLIES WITH RULES ADOPTED BY THE SECRETARY OF STATE; OR

(C) AN IDENTITY VERIFICATION BY A TRUSTED THIRD PARTY THAT COMPLIES WITH RULES ADOPTED BY THE SECRETARY OF STATE; OR

(III) ANY OTHER METHOD THAT COMPLIES WITH RULES ADOPTED BY THE SECRETARY OF STATE.

(7) WITHOUT LIMITING THE AUTHORITY OF A NOTARY PUBLIC UNDER SECTION 24-21-508 TO REFUSE TO PERFORM A NOTARIAL ACT, A NOTARY PUBLIC MAY REFUSE TO PERFORM A NOTARIAL ACT UNDER THIS SECTION IF THE NOTARY PUBLIC IS NOT SATISFIED THAT THE REQUIREMENTS OF THIS SECTION ARE MET.

(8) THE CERTIFICATE OF NOTARIAL ACT FOR A REMOTE NOTARIZATION MUST, IN ADDITION TO COMPLYING WITH THE REQUIREMENTS OF SECTION 24-21-515, INDICATE THAT THE NOTARIAL ACT WAS PERFORMED USING AUDIO-VIDEO COMMUNICATION TECHNOLOGY.

(9) (a) A NOTARY PUBLIC SHALL CREATE AN AUDIO-VIDEO RECORDING OF A REMOTE NOTARIZATION IF:

(I) THE NOTARY PUBLIC FIRST DISCLOSES TO THE REMOTELY LOCATED INDIVIDUAL THE FACT OF THE RECORDING AND THE DETAILS OF ITS INTENDED STORAGE, INCLUDING WHERE AND FOR HOW LONG IT WILL BE STORED;

(II) THE REMOTELY LOCATED INDIVIDUAL EXPLICITLY CONSENTS TO BOTH THE RECORDING AND THE STORAGE OF THE RECORDING; AND

(III) THE RECORDING IS STORED AND SECURED IN COMPLIANCE WITH RULES ADOPTED BY THE SECRETARY OF STATE.

(b) THE AUDIO-VIDEO RECORDING REQUIRED BY THIS SUBSECTION (9) MUST BE IN ADDITION TO THE JOURNAL ENTRY FOR THE NOTARIAL ACT WHERE REQUIRED BY SECTION 24-21-519. THE RECORDING MUST INCLUDE THE INFORMATION DESCRIBED IN THIS SUBSECTION (9)(b). A NOTARY PUBLIC SHALL MAKE A GOOD-FAITH EFFORT TO NOT INCLUDE ANY OTHER INFORMATION ON THE RECORDING. ANY OTHER INFORMATION INCLUDED ON THE RECORDING IS NOT ADMISSIBLE IN ANY COURT OF LAW, LEGAL PROCEEDING, OR ADMINISTRATIVE HEARING FOR ANY PURPOSE, NOR IS THE INFORMATION ADMISSIBLE IN ANY PROCEEDING IN ANY OTHER COURT OF LAW, LEGAL PROCEEDING, OR ADMINISTRATIVE HEARING IF COLORADO LAW APPLIES WITH RESPECT TO REMOTE NOTARIZATION. THE RECORDING MUST INCLUDE:

(I) AT THE COMMENCEMENT OF THE RECORDING, A RECITATION BY THE NOTARY PUBLIC OF INFORMATION SUFFICIENT TO IDENTIFY THE NOTARIAL ACT, INCLUDING THE NAME OF THE NOTARY PUBLIC, THE DATE AND TIME OF THE NOTARIAL ACT, A DESCRIPTION OF THE NATURE OF THE DOCUMENT OR DOCUMENTS TO WHICH THE NOTARIAL ACT IS TO RELATE, THE IDENTITY OF THE REMOTELY LOCATED INDIVIDUAL WHOSE SIGNATURE IS TO BE THE SUBJECT OF THE NOTARIAL ACT AND OF ANY PERSON WHO WILL ACT AS A CREDIBLE WITNESS TO IDENTIFY THE INDIVIDUAL SIGNER, AND THE METHOD OR METHODS BY WHICH THE REMOTELY LOCATED INDIVIDUAL AND ANY CREDIBLE WITNESS WILL BE IDENTIFIED TO THE NOTARY PUBLIC;

(II) A DECLARATION BY THE REMOTELY LOCATED INDIVIDUAL THAT THE INDIVIDUAL'S SIGNATURE ON THE RECORD IS KNOWINGLY AND VOLUNTARILY MADE;

(III) IF THE REMOTELY LOCATED INDIVIDUAL FOR WHOM THE NOTARIAL ACT IS BEING PERFORMED IS IDENTIFIED BY PERSONAL KNOWLEDGE, AN EXPLANATION BY THE NOTARY PUBLIC AS TO HOW THE NOTARY PUBLIC KNOWS THE REMOTELY LOCATED INDIVIDUAL AND HOW LONG THE NOTARY PUBLIC HAS KNOWN THE REMOTELY LOCATED INDIVIDUAL;

(IV) IF THE REMOTELY LOCATED INDIVIDUAL FOR WHOM THE NOTARIAL ACT IS BEING PERFORMED IS IDENTIFIED BY A CREDIBLE WITNESS:

(A) A STATEMENT BY THE NOTARY PUBLIC AS TO HOW THE NOTARY PUBLIC KNOWS THE CREDIBLE WITNESS AND HOW LONG THE NOTARY PUBLIC HAS KNOWN THE CREDIBLE WITNESS; AND

(B) AN EXPLANATION BY THE CREDIBLE WITNESS AS TO HOW THE CREDIBLE WITNESS KNOWS THE REMOTELY LOCATED INDIVIDUAL AND HOW LONG THE CREDIBLE WITNESS HAS KNOWN THE REMOTELY LOCATED INDIVIDUAL; AND

(V) THE STATEMENTS, ACTS, AND CONDUCT NECESSARY TO PERFORM THE REQUESTED NOTARIAL ACT OR SUPERVISION OF SIGNING OR WITNESSING OF THE SUBJECT RECORD.

(c) THE PROVISIONS OF SECTION 24-21-519 THAT RELATE TO THE SECURITY, INSPECTION, COPYING, AND RETENTION AND DISPOSITION OF A NOTARY PUBLIC'S JOURNAL APPLY EQUALLY TO THE SECURITY, INSPECTION, COPYING, AND RETENTION AND DISPOSITION OF AUDIO-VIDEO RECORDINGS ALLOWED BY THIS SECTION.

(d) THE FAILURE OF A NOTARY PUBLIC TO PERFORM A DUTY OR MEET A REQUIREMENT SPECIFIED IN THIS SUBSECTION (9) DOES NOT INVALIDATE A REMOTE NOTARIZATION PERFORMED BY THE NOTARY PUBLIC. A NOTARY PUBLIC IS NOT LIABLE TO ANY PERSON FOR DAMAGES CLAIMED TO ARISE FROM A FAILURE TO PERFORM A DUTY OR MEET A REQUIREMENT SPECIFIED IN SUBSECTION (9)(b) OF THIS SECTION.

(10) REGARDLESS OF THE PHYSICAL LOCATION OF THE REMOTELY LOCATED INDIVIDUAL AT THE TIME OF THE NOTARIAL ACT, THE VALIDITY OF A REMOTE NOTARIZATION PERFORMED BY A NOTARY IN THIS STATE IS GOVERNED BY THE LAWS OF THIS STATE, INCLUDING ANY RULES ADOPTED BY THE SECRETARY OF STATE PURSUANT TO THIS PART 5.

(11) To BE ELIGIBLE FOR APPROVAL BY THE SECRETARY OF STATE UNDER SECTION 24-21-527 (1)(h), A PROVIDER OF A REMOTE NOTARIZATION SYSTEM OR STORAGE SYSTEM MUST:

(a) CERTIFY TO THE SECRETARY OF STATE THAT THE PROVIDER AND THE SYSTEM COMPLY WITH THE REQUIREMENTS OF THIS SECTION AND THE RULES ADOPTED UNDER SECTION 24-21-527;

(b) MAINTAIN A USUAL PLACE OF BUSINESS IN THIS STATE OR, IF A FOREIGN ENTITY, APPOINT AND MAINTAIN A REGISTERED AGENT, IN ACCORDANCE WITH SECTION 7-90-701 BY FILING A STATEMENT OF FOREIGN ENTITY AUTHORITY IN ACCORDANCE WITH SECTION 7-90-803, WITH AUTHORITY TO ACCEPT SERVICE OF PROCESS IN CONNECTION WITH A CIVIL ACTION OR OTHER PROCEEDING; AND

(c) NOT USE, SELL, OR OFFER TO SELL TO ANOTHER PERSON OR TRANSFER TO ANOTHER PERSON FOR USE OR SALE ANY PERSONAL INFORMATION OBTAINED UNDER THIS SECTION THAT IDENTIFIES A REMOTELY LOCATED INDIVIDUAL, A WITNESS TO A REMOTE NOTARIZATION, OR A PERSON NAMED IN A RECORD PRESENTED FOR REMOTE NOTARIZATION, EXCEPT:

(I) AS NECESSARY TO FACILITATE PERFORMANCE OF A NOTARIAL ACT;

(II) To EFFECT, ADMINISTER, ENFORCE, SERVICE, OR PROCESS A RECORD PROVIDED BY OR ON BEHALF OF THE INDIVIDUAL OR THE TRANSACTION OF WHICH THE RECORD IS A PART;

(III) IN ACCORDANCE WITH THIS PART 5 AND THE RULES ADOPTED PURSUANT TO THIS PART 5 OR OTHER APPLICABLE FEDERAL, STATE, OR LOCAL LAW, OR TO COMPLY WITH A LAWFUL SUBPOENA OR COURT ORDER; OR

(IV) IN CONNECTION WITH A PROPOSED OR ACTUAL SALE, MERGER, TRANSFER, OR EXCHANGE OF ALL OR A PORTION OF A BUSINESS OR OPERATING UNIT OF THE PROVIDER, IF THE PERSONAL INFORMATION CONCERNS ONLY CUSTOMERS OF THE BUSINESS OR UNIT AND THE TRANSFEREE AGREES TO COMPLY WITH THE RESTRICTIONS SET FORTH IN THIS SUBSECTION (11).

(12) SUBJECT TO APPLICABLE LAW OTHER THAN THIS ARTICLE 21, IF A RECORD IS PRIVILEGED PURSUANT TO SECTION 13-90-107 (1)(b), THE CORRESPONDING ELECTRONIC RECORD SECURED AND STORED BY THE REMOTE NOTARIZATION SYSTEM AS PROVIDED IN THIS ARTICLE 21 REMAINS PRIVILEGED.

SECTION 5. In Colorado Revised Statutes, 24-21-515, **amend** (3)(d) and (4) as follows:

24-21-515. Certificate of notarial act. (3) A certificate of a notarial act is sufficient if it meets the requirements of subsections (1) and (2) of this section and:

(d) Sets forth the actions of the notarial officer and the actions THAT are sufficient to meet the requirements of the notarial act as provided in sections 24-21-505, 24-21-506, and 24-21-507 AND, IF APPLICABLE, SECTION 24-21-514.5 or law of this state other than this part 5.

(4) By executing a certificate of a notarial act, a notarial officer certifies that the officer has complied with the requirements and made the determinations specified in sections 24-21-504, 24-21-505, and 24-21-506 AND, IF APPLICABLE, SECTION 24-21-514.5.

SECTION 6. In Colorado Revised Statutes, 24-21-519, **amend** (2) as follows:

24-21-519. Journal. (2) (a) A journal may be created on a tangible medium or in an electronic format. If a journal is maintained on a tangible medium, it must be a permanent, bound register with numbered pages. If a journal is maintained in an electronic format, it must be in a permanent, tamper-evident electronic format complying with the rules of the secretary of state.

(b) A NOTARY PUBLIC WHO PERFORMS A REMOTE NOTARIZATION SHALL MAINTAIN A JOURNAL IN AN ELECTRONIC FORMAT WITH REGARD TO EACH REMOTE NOTARIZATION.

SECTION 7. In Colorado Revised Statutes, 24-21-527, **amend** (1)(e); and **add** (1)(g), (1)(h), and (3) as follows:

24-21-527. Rules - definitions - repeal. (1) The secretary of state may adopt rules to implement this part 5 in accordance with article 4 of this title 24. Rules adopted regarding the performance of notarial acts with respect to electronic records may not require, or accord greater legal status or effect to, the implementation or application of a specific technology or technical specification. The rules may:

(e) Include provisions to prevent fraud or mistake in the performance of notarial acts; and

(g) PRESCRIBE THE MANNER OF PERFORMING NOTARIAL ACTS USING AUDIO-VIDEO COMMUNICATION TECHNOLOGY, INCLUDING PROVISIONS TO ENSURE THE SECURITY, INTEGRITY, AND ACCESSIBILITY OF RECORDS RELATING TO THOSE ACTS; AND

(h) PRESCRIBE REQUIREMENTS FOR THE APPROVAL AND USE OF REMOTE NOTARIZATION SYSTEMS AND STORAGE SYSTEMS.

(3) (a) AS USED IN THIS SUBSECTION (3):

(I) "INTERIM PERIOD" MEANS THE PERIOD BEGINNING ON MARCH 30, 2020, AND ENDING ON DECEMBER 31, 2020.

(II) "TEMPORARY RULE" MEANS RULE 5 OF THE NOTARY PROGRAM RULES AS ADOPTED BY THE SECRETARY OF STATE EFFECTIVE MARCH 30, 2020, AND PUBLISHED AT 8 CCR 1505-11, AND ANY ANALOGOUS SUCCESSOR EMERGENCY RULE OF THE NOTARY PROGRAM THAT AUTHORIZES REMOTE NOTARIZATIONS.

(b) DURING THE INTERIM PERIOD:

(I) A NOTARY PUBLIC COMMISSIONED BY THE SECRETARY OF STATE MAY PERFORM NOTARIAL ACTS WITH RESPECT TO A REMOTELY LOCATED INDIVIDUAL USING AUDIO-VIDEO COMMUNICATION IN ACCORDANCE WITH, AND SUBJECT TO THE LIMITATIONS AND RESTRICTIONS SET FORTH IN, THE TEMPORARY RULE; AND

(II) INSOFAR AS IT RELATES TO ANY NOTARIAL ACT PERMITTED BY THE TEMPORARY RULE AND PERFORMED DURING THE INTERIM PERIOD, ANY REQUIREMENT IN THIS PART 5 OR TITLE 38 THAT AN INDIVIDUAL MAKING A STATEMENT OR EXECUTING A SIGNATURE APPEAR PERSONALLY BEFORE A NOTARIAL OFFICER IS SATISFIED BY THE PROCEDURES SPECIFIED IN AND PERMITTED BY THE TEMPORARY RULE.

(c) THE SECRETARY OF STATE MAY AMEND THE TEMPORARY RULE IN ACCORDANCE WITH ARTICLE 4 OF THIS TITLE 24, BUT THE AMENDMENT MUST NOT PERMIT THE PERFORMANCE OF A REMOTE NOTARIZATION WITH RESPECT TO A RECORD DESCRIBED IN SECTION 5.2.2 OF THE TEMPORARY RULE OTHER THAN IN ACCORDANCE WITH THE PROVISIONS OF THE TEMPORARY RULE AS IT EXISTED ON THE EFFECTIVE DATE OF THIS SUBSECTION (3).

(d) A NOTARIAL ACT PERFORMED DURING THE INTERIM PERIOD WITH RESPECT TO A REMOTELY LOCATED INDIVIDUAL THAT COMPLIED WITH THE TEMPORARY RULE IS NOT INVALID DUE TO THE LACK OF EXPRESS STATUTORY AUTHORITY FOR THE NOTARIAL ACT.

(e) THE SECRETARY OF STATE SHALL UPDATE THE APPLICABLE JOINT COMMITTEE OF REFERENCE DURING THE DEPARTMENT OF STATE'S 2020 PRESENTATION MADE PURSUANT TO SECTION 2-7-203 REGARDING THE IMPLEMENTATION OF THIS SUBSECTION (3).

(f) SUBSECTIONS (3)(b), (3)(c), AND (3)(e) OF THIS SECTION AND THIS SUBSECTION (3)(f) ARE REPEALED, EFFECTIVE DECEMBER 31, 2020.

SECTION 8. In Colorado Revised Statutes, 10-11-122, **add** (4) as follows:

10-11-122. Title commitments - rules. (4) (a) IF A TITLE INSURANCE AGENT OR TITLE INSURANCE COMPANY IS REQUIRED TO PROVIDE THE STATEMENT REQUIRED BY SUBSECTION (1) OF THIS SECTION, THE AGENT OR COMPANY SHALL ALSO PROVIDE A STATEMENT SUBSTANTIALLY AS FOLLOWS:

> COLORADO NOTARIES MAY REMOTELY NOTARIZE REAL ESTATE DEEDS AND OTHER DOCUMENTS USING REAL-TIME AUDIO-VIDEO COMMUNICATION TECHNOLOGY. YOU MAY CHOOSE NOT TO USE REMOTE NOTARIZATION FOR ANY DOCUMENT.

(b) FAILURE OF A PERSON TO PROVIDE THE STATEMENT REQUIRED BY THIS SUBSECTION (4) DOES NOT SUBJECT THE PERSON TO ANY LIABILITY UNDER THIS ARTICLE 11 OR TO THE PENALTY PROVISIONS OF SECTION 10-3-111 AND DOES NOT AFFECT OR INVALIDATE ANY PROVISIONS OF THE COMMITMENT FOR TITLE INSURANCE.

SECTION 9. Appropriation. (1) For the 2020-21 state fiscal year, $132,795 is appropriated to the department of state. This appropriation is from the department of state cash fund created in section 24-21-104 (3)(b), C.R.S. To implement this act, the department may use this appropriation as follows:

(a) $57,910 for use by the business and licensing division for personal services, which amount is based on an assumption that the division will require an additional 1.1 FTE;

(b) $7,685 for use by the business and licensing division for operating expenses; and

(c) $67,200 for use by the information technology division for personal services.

SECTION 10. Effective date - applicability. (1) This act:

(a) Takes effect upon passage; except that sections 1 through 6 and 8 of this act take effect December 31, 2020; and

(b) Applies to conduct occurring on or after March 30, 2020.

SECTION 11. Safety clause. The general assembly hereby finds, determines, and declares that this act is necessary for the immediate preservation of the public peace, health, or safety.

Leroy M. Garcia	KC Becker
PRESIDENT OF	SPEAKER OF THE HOUSE
THE SENATE	OF REPRESENTATIVES
Cindi L. Markwell	Robin Jones
SECRETARY OF	CHIEF CLERK OF THE HOUSE
THE SENATE	OF REPRESENTATIVES

APPROVED June 26, 2020 at 1:07 PM

(Date and Time)

Jared S. Polis
GOVERNOR OF THE STATE OF COLORADO

About the NNA

Since 1957, the National Notary Association has been committed to serving and educating the nation's Notaries. During that time, the NNA® has become known as the most trusted source of information for and about Notaries and Notary laws, rules and best practices.

The NNA serves Notaries through its NationalNotary.org website, social media, publications, annual conferences, seminars, online training and the NNA® Hotline, which offers immediate answers to specific questions about notarization.

In addition, the NNA offers the highest quality professional supplies, including official seals and stamps, recordkeeping journals, Notary certificates and Notary bonds.

Though dedicated primarily to educating and assisting Notaries, the NNA supports implementing effective Notary laws and informing the public about the Notary's vital role in today's society.

To learn more about the National Notary Association, visit NationalNotary.org. ■

Index

A

Acknowledgments 22–25
Address change 7
Advertising 34–35
Affidavits 27–28
Affirmations 24–26
Alternative communication
   methods 13
Apostilles 19
Application 3–4
Audio-video communication
   quality considerations 47
Authentication 19–20
Authorization to perform RON 46
Authorized acts 21–22
Awareness 9

B

Beneficial interest 16–17
Blank documents 15
Bond, Notary 5–6

C

Certificate, Notary 39–42
Certificate of remote notarial
   act 50
Civil lawsuit 56
Commission recording 6

Copy certifications 26–28
Credible identifying witness 10–12

D

Death of Notary 7
Depositions 27–28
Disciplinary action 55–56
Disqualifying interest 16–17

E

Electronic notarization 44–45
Errors and omissions insurance 5

F

Family members, notarizing for 16
Faxes 20
Fees 32–33
Financial interest 16–17
Fines 51–55
Foreign languages 9, 17–18

I

Identification of the remotely
   located signer 47–48
Identifying document signers 9
Immigration 18
Incomplete documents 15

J

Journal of notarial acts 35–38
Jurat 28-29
Jurisdiction 6–7

L

Liability of Notary 56
Location of Notary and
 signer 46–47
Locus sigilli (or L.S.) 43

M

Minors, notarizing for 13–14
Misconduct 51–55

N

Name change 7
Nondisciplinary actions 55–56
Notarial acts 21–35
Notario publico 55

O

Oaths 24–26

P

Penalties 51–55
Personal appearance 8
Personal knowledge of identity 10
Photocopies 20
Prohibited acts 51–52
Prohibited documents 50
Proof of execution by subscribing
 witness 30–32

R

Reappointment 6–7
Reasonable care 16
Refusal of appointment 53–55
Refusal of service 15–16
Remote online notarization 46–50
Remote online notarization
 defined 46
Resignation of appointment 7–8
Revocation of appointment 53–55

Right to a hearing 55
RON record-keeping
 requirements 48–49

S

Satisfactory evidence 28
Signature 37
Signature by mark 12
Signature by proxy 13
Stamp, Notary 42–43

T

Telephone notarization 8
Term of office 6

U

Unauthorized acts 22
Unauthorized practice of law .. 17–18

V

Verification on oath or
 affirmation 28–29

W

Willingness 8
Wills 18–19

Index | 107

Notes